W9-CSB-675

The Multimedia Writing Toolkit

The Multimedia Writing Toolkit demonstrates how, by drawing on students' interest in and familiarity with technology, you can integrate multimedia to maximize the potential of writing instruction. In eight concise chapters, author Sean Ruday identifies and describes simple, common forms of multimedia that upper elementary and middle school students can use to improve their argument, informational, and narrative writing and critical thinking. You'll learn how to:

- Incorporate multimedia into argument, informational, and narrative writing through students' use of video topic trailers, online discussion boards, webpages, and more.
- Evaluate students on effective use of multimedia through easy-to-follow rubrics and explicitly articulated learning goals.
- Understand more fully the key forms of multimedia through user-friendly overviews and explanations; you don't need to be a "techie" teacher to use these strategies!
- Overcome possible obstacles to the integration of multimedia in the classroom by learning from the author's concrete, first-hand examples and instructional recommendations.

This book is complete with resources designed to provide you with extra support, including reproducible classroom-appropriate charts and forms, links to key web-based content discussed in the book, and a guide for teachers and administrators interested in using the book for group-based professional development. With *The Multimedia Writing Toolkit*, you'll have a clear game plan for encouraging your students to become more engaged, technologically savvy learners.

Bonus: Blank templates of the handouts are available as printable eResources on our website (www.routledge.com/9781138200111).

Sean Ruday is Assistant Professor of English Education at Longwood University. He is also the author of *The Argument Writing Toolkit* (Grades 6–8), *The Informational Writing Toolkit* (Grades 3–5), *The Narrative Writing Toolkit* (Grades 3–8), and *The Common Core Grammar Toolkit* books (Grades 3–5 and 6–8).

Other Toolkit Books Available from Sean Ruday

(www.routledge.com/eyeoneducation)

The Argument Writing Toolkit
Using Mentor Texts in Grades 6–8

The Informational Writing Toolkit
Using Mentor Texts in Grades 3–5

The Narrative Writing Toolkit
Using Mentor Texts in Grades 3–8

The Common Core Grammar Toolkit
Using Mentor Texts to Teach the Language Standards in Grades 6–8

The Common Core Grammar Toolkit
Using Mentor Texts to Teach the Language Standards in Grades 3–5

The Multimedia Writing Toolkit

Helping Students Incorporate Graphics and Videos for Authentic Purposes, Grades 3–8

Sean Ruday

Routledge
Taylor & Francis Group

NEW YORK AND LONDON

DISCARDED

SCHENECTADY CO PUBLIC LIBRARY

First published 2017
by Routledge
711 Third Avenue, New York, NY 10017

and by Routledge
2 Park Square, Milton Park, Abingdon, Oxon, OX14 4RN

Routledge is an imprint of the Taylor & Francis Group, an informa business

© 2017 Taylor & Francis

The right of Sean Ruday to be identified as author of this work has been asserted by him in accordance with sections 77 and 78 of the Copyright, Designs and Patents Act 1988.

All rights reserved. The purchase of this copyright material confers the right on the purchasing institution to photocopy or download pages which bear the eResources icon and a copyright line at the bottom of the page. No other parts of this book may be reprinted or reproduced or utilised in any form or by any electronic, mechanical, or other means, now known or hereafter invented, including photocopying and recording, or in any information storage or retrieval system, without permission in writing from the publishers.

Trademark notice: Product or corporate names may be trademarks or registered trademarks, and are used only for identification and explanation without intent to infringe.

Library of Congress Cataloging in Publication Data
A catalog record for this book has been requested

ISBN: 978-1-138-20010-4 (hbk)
ISBN: 978-1-138-20011-1 (pbk)
ISBN: 978-1-315-51521-2 (ebk)

Typeset in Palatino and Formata
by Apex CoVantage, LLC

Contents

Meet the Author

Sean Ruday is an Assistant Professor of English Education at Longwood University. He began his teaching career at a public school in Brooklyn, New York, and has taught English and language arts in New York, Massachusetts, and Virginia. Sean is a co-president of the Assembly for the Teaching of English Grammar—a grammar-focused affiliate of the National Council of Teachers of English. He is the founder and editor of the *Journal of Literacy Innovation* and editor of the *Virginia English Journal*. Some publications in which his articles have appeared are *Journal of Teaching Writing, Journal of Language and Literacy Education, Contemporary Issues in Technology and Teacher Education,* and the *Yearbook of the Literacy Research Association.* His professional website is http://seanruday.weebly.com. You can follow him on Twitter @SeanRuday. This is his sixth book with Routledge Eye on Education.

eResources

The appendices of this book can also be downloaded and printed for classroom use. You can access these downloads by visiting the book product page on our website: http://www.routledge.com/products/ 978-1-138-20011-1. Then click on the tab that says "eResources," and select the files. They will begin downloading to your computer.

Acknowledgments

I am extremely appreciative of the hard work and insightful ideas of Longwood University student Ashlyn Kemp, who worked as research apprentice on this project. Be on the lookout for Ashlyn as she prepares to take the education world by storm!

I greatly appreciate the teachers who shared their thoughts with me and gave me the opportunity to work with them and their students. Similarly, I am grateful for the wonderful students in the classes described in this book who eagerly dove into the ideas and tools of multimedia integration. Special thanks to the phenomenal Sawyer Ruday, whose skills are prominently featured in this text.

I am very thankful for this book's editor, Lauren Davis: thank you for the constant support and for helping me launch my writing career!

I would like to thank my parents, Bob and Joyce Ruday, for all that they have done for me. I also want to thank my wife, Clare Ruday, who brightens my life by bringing humor and happiness to it.

Reimagining Writing Instruction

It's a sunny winter morning in a seventh-grade English class and the room hums with the energy and excitement that accompanies student engagement; the students are, in their words, "changing the game" by incorporating multimedia into the writing projects on which they've been working. These students recently took photos and created videos depicting real-world scenarios and situations to use as supporting evidence in their argument essays. Today, they're creating their own websites that they will use to share their essays with authentic audiences.

"This is totally changing the game," explains a student excited by these technological integrations. "Writing in school is never like this. It's usually totally different. We never use technology except for things like PowerPoint and typing our papers. Now, we get to actually use technology in our writing by including photos we take and videos we make that go along with the arguments in our essays. It's really fun and, I think, makes the essay more interesting, too."

"Plus," interjects another student, "we usually just write stuff that [their teacher] reads. Now, we're making websites that can get read by a lot of people. My argument essay's about why our school needs to take longer field trips, like overnight ones to farther away places. Now that I'm making a website, I can get a lot more people to read my ideas than just [the teacher]."

Later that day, in a professional development session with the school's faculty, I asked what the teachers noticed about incorporating multimedia into their writing instruction. I was thrilled that many teachers commented that this instructional approach both engaged their students and facilitated a purposeful use of technology. Kimberly, a sixth-grade teacher, identified each of these ideas while describing her experience: "There's no question the kids are more into writing when we incorporate multimedia, which is definitely great—we want our students to be engaged—but the main way this has helped me as a teacher is it's helped me use technology with a purpose, with a reason behind *why* I'm using it. I feel like so much of the time, I'm just using technology because someone says to use technology more, but I don't really know if it's making my teaching even better. When I help my kids incorporate multimedia into their writing, I know exactly *why* I'm doing it. It's not like when I just use the Smart Board because someone says, 'Hey, Kim, here's a Smart Board. Now use it.'"

Kimberly's response, which elicited both laughter and applause from the other teachers in the room, illuminated an important point: technology has the power to engage students, but teachers need to understand how to effectively integrate it in ways that enhance their instruction so that they can avoid using technology for technology's sake. I decided to write this book to provide a resource for elementary and middle school teachers who are looking to do what Kimberly described: integrate multimedia and technology into their instruction in ways that engage students *and* represent the best ways to achieve important learning goals.

This introductory chapter is divided into four sections, each addressing a key component of the book's approach:

- ◆ Why integrating multimedia can maximize the potential of writing instruction
- ◆ What to watch out for when integrating multimedia into writing instruction
- ◆ Why you don't need be a "techie" teacher to integrate multimedia into writing instruction
- ◆ What to expect in this book

Why Integrating Multimedia Can Maximize the Potential of Writing Instruction

The incorporation of multimedia into teaching writing can maximize the potential of writing instruction by drawing on students' knowledge of and familiarity with multiple literacies (Wolsey & Grisham, 2012). Think back to the student quotations in the preceding vignette: one student explained that he enjoyed integrating multimedia into argument writing because it makes the writing process more enjoyable and helps create a higher-quality final product. When I followed up with the student about his comments, he explained that multimedia-infused writing instruction is aligned with the kind of written works he often reads: "I read a lot of sports articles online, like on ESPN.com. In these articles, there are usually pictures and videos that go along with what's written. I think articles with these things are just more interesting and give more information. That's what I read, so that's what I'm used to." This comment sheds light on the role that multimedia plays in many of the high-interest articles that our students encounter. While we writing teachers should help students understand the power of the written word, it is also in our best interest to understand the potential impact of multimedia on our students' writing experiences (Frey,

Fisher, & Gonzalez, 2010). Throughout this book, we'll consider ways to help students integrate multimedia into their works while still valuing the fundamental skills needed to help them be successful writers.

Multimedia can also have a positive impact on students' writings through the opportunity to express meaningful ideas authentically. A major reason many literacy teachers have integrated technology into instruction is that it makes the process of students sharing ideas easier (Ruday, 2011). Online discussion boards, webpages, and blogs allow students to share their works and ideas with audiences other than their teacher, which can motivate students by giving them authentic audiences for their works. For example, the middle school student who made a webpage to share his argument that his school should take longer field trips was excited by the chance to share his work with a larger audience: "That makes it feel like what you're writing really means something," he explained. "When you only write for the teacher, it just stops there. When you write and post things online, you can share your ideas with more people and get them on board." The student continued to comment on the feeling of relevance that sharing his work online provided: "I feel like I'm doing something for real now [by creating a webpage to share these ideas]. It's different from the usual writing you do in school that doesn't really seem real." These comments struck me because of their thoughtful insight: this student noted his belief that the essays he typically writes for school don't seem especially meaningful because they're not shared with a larger audience. In contrast, taking advantage of possible ways to convey his thoughts with other interested individuals provided a motivational component, unlike what he typically experienced.

Another key benefit of incorporating multimedia into writing instruction is the preparation it provides students for the kinds of writing they'll be asked to do in their futures. While it's wonderful that integrating technology appeals to students' interests, it's just as important to note that multimedia-infused writing is where the world of writing and media is going and will continue to go. Similarly, the multimedia inclusion strategies described in this book provide concrete ways to help teachers meet the Common Core State Standards' media literacy components. These standards, designed to help enhance students' college and career readiness, call for students to use technology to produce writing and collaborate with others (Common Core State Standards, 2010). The strategies and tactics for multimedia incorporation described in this book will give you concrete ways to help prepare students for these aspects of their futures.

What to Watch Out for When Integrating Multimedia into Writing Instruction

While the inclusion of multimedia can have a number of positive impacts on writing instruction, teachers should still be aware of potential issues that can emerge. Problems can arise when students are overreliant on multimedia in their writings and don't incorporate it strategically. For example, I recently met with a student whose argument essay on the benefits of children participating in theater used an excessive amount of images and videos. The student selected and integrated these multimedia with good intentions but relied too much on them and not enough on his writing to convey his ideas. In my conversation with this student, I talked to him about the importance of multimedia supplementing the text of a piece of writing but not overtaking it: "You want to be sure the multimedia is playing a supporting role. The written word is the main star of an essay; multimedia like images and videos can be great additions, but they have to stay in that supporting role. The essay won't be as effective if the multimedia overshadows the written word."

This example illustrates the importance of using multimedia strategically, with a clear understanding of the benefits it provides and the learning goals it helps achieve (Young & Bush, 2004). Since multimedia has the potential to engage students and foster connections to their out-of-school lives (Lenhart, Madden, & Hitlin, 2005), it is easy for "multimedia-enhanced writing" to become "writing with too much multimedia in it." We writing teachers can guard against potential overuses of multimedia by helping our students understand the importance of using technological innovations carefully and critically. After I met with the student who used an excessive amount of images and videos in his argument essay, I spoke with the whole class about the strategic use of multimedia: "Like we've been talking about lately, multimedia can definitely be a great way to enhance a piece of writing. However, it has a kind of downside as well—it can be overused. Sometimes writers use multimedia so much that the images, videos, and graphics overwhelm the written words, and readers don't even feel like they're reading a piece of writing anymore. When you're incorporating multimedia into your writing, make sure you do it carefully so that it supports important information in your work without overshadowing it."

Why You Don't Need to Be a "Techie" Teacher to Integrate Multimedia into Writing Instruction

When I first spoke to teachers about the idea of integrating multimedia into writing instruction, I encountered some technology-oriented resistance: "I'm not a 'techie,'" a sixth-grade teacher asserted. "I'm a teacher, not a technology expert. I'm worried I'll get overwhelmed teaching my students to use multimedia in their writing."

"Those are definitely important concerns," I responded. "There's so much technology out there today that it can definitely be overwhelming. It seems like there are so many programs and apps out there that some people are using in their teaching. The recommendations I'm going to share with you, though, don't require you to be a 'techie' to effectively implement them into your instruction. They're really user-friendly and relate to a lot of forms of technology students already know how to use or are easily able to learn."

As I shared with this teacher, the forms of multimedia described in this book are designed to be easy to integrate and related to students' prior knowledge and/or zones of proximal development. When deciding whether or not to include each form of multimedia described in this book, I asked myself three questions: (1) Can this multimedia improve student writing? (2) Is this multimedia easy for most teachers to understand and use? (3) Does this multimedia reflect material students may have encountered outside of school or are likely to understand? I only included forms of multimedia in this book for which I answered "yes" to all three questions; I wanted to make sure that the multimedia I discussed with my students and with this book's readers has the potential to make writing better, is straightforward enough that teachers can use it in their classes without feeling overwhelmed by technological programs and innovations, and is either familiar to students or within their zones of proximal development.

I believe that technology that aligns with all three of these criteria provides the greatest benefit possible to teachers and students, as it has the potential to be useful, accessible, and engaging. For example, Chapter Four of this book describes the use of images and figures in informational writing to aid comprehension and illustrate concepts, explaining what this multimedia form is, why it can enhance a piece of writing, and how it can be integrated into the classroom. These explanations are designed to be useful to all teachers, no matter their familiarity with technology, as this book's focus is on using multimedia in strategic ways that enhance student writing and keep students engaged, not on using technology for the sake of doing so.

What to Expect in This Book

This book identifies and describes key forms of multimedia that upper-elementary and middle school students can strategically integrate into their argument, informational, and narrative writing. It discusses specific, classroom-ready practices teachers can use to help their students implement these components into their works and is divided into five sections:

◆ Section One focuses on incorporating multimedia into argument writing. The first chapter in this section deals with students using photos and videos as supporting evidence for their arguments, while the second addresses students connecting to authentic audiences through websites they create.

◆ Section Two describes incorporating multimedia into informational writing. One chapter in this section discusses students creating video topic trailers that introduce key points they develop in their essays, while the next chapter focuses on students using images and figures that aid readers' comprehension and illustrate concepts that are important in their works.

◆ Section Three addresses incorporating multimedia into narrative writing. This section's initial chapter describes students using images, videos, and audio files as tools for characterization; the second chapter in this section focuses on students incorporating multimedia that conveys thematic elements, such as images that highlight key messages, themes, and ideas in narratives.

   ◆ For consistency and ease of use, I've organized each chapter in Sections One, Two, and Three into the following sections:

      ◆ "What Is It?" This section provides an overview and explanation of the multimedia form described in the chapter. The introductory information provided here helps ensure readers' understanding of each chapter's focal strategy.

      ◆ "Why Is It Beneficial?" This section discusses why the multimedia discussed in the chapter can help enhance student writing. The information here is meant to provide a rationale for using the multimedia form on which the chapter focuses. This is the chapter from which you'll draw if anyone asks why your students are incorporating a particular technological innovation into their writing.

      ◆ "A Classroom Snapshot." This section describes my experiences teaching students in elementary or middle school how to incorporate the multimedia described in the chapter into their writing. I've included these snapshots so you can see how I taught my students to use multimedia to enhance their works and learn from these concrete examples as you work with your own students.

      ◆ "Instructional Recommendations." Each chapter closes with specific recommendations for you to keep in mind when helping your students incorporate specific forms of multimedia into their own works.

◆ Section Four focuses on "Putting It Together." One chapter in this section features strategies and easy-to-follow rubrics to use when assessing your students' integration of multimedia into their writing, while the second chapter in the section contains final thoughts and tips that will help you put the ideas and recommendations described in this book into action in your own classroom.

◆ Section Five contains the following resources designed to provide you with extra support as you put this book's ideas into practice:

  ◆ The book's reference list
  ◆ Appendix A, featuring reproducible charts and forms you can use in your classroom
  ◆ Appendix B, containing a guide for teachers and administrators interested in using this book for a professional book study
  ◆ Appendix C, which contains links to key web-based content discussed in this book

The idea of incorporating multimedia into student writing is complex: on one hand, the use of multimedia can help engage students by connecting with their interest in using various technological innovations to communicate (Lenhart, Madden, & Hitlin, 2005) and allowing them to share their ideas with audiences in new ways (Ruday, 2011). On the other hand, technology is sometimes overly relied on and used simply for the sake of doing so, not because it is the best way of reaching particular learning goals (Young & Bush, 2004). We as teachers can address these complex benefits and challenges by helping our students implement relevant, useful multimedia forms that can enhance their works and engage them in their learning.

The book you hold in your hands will give you a game plan for helping your students strategically and effectively incorporate multimedia in their argument, informational, and narrative works. While I've organized the multimedia tools in this book based on certain genres, it's important to note that these tools can be applied to other genres as well; for example, video topic trailers, which I describe as aligned with informational writing, can also be used in conjunction with argument and narrative writing. I recommend not only using the tools in this book when teaching the genre under which I've listed each tool but also considering ways to apply them to other genres. For example, in addition to using student-created websites when helping your students share their argument essays with interested parties, also consider other genres to which you might apply this use of multimedia. As you examine these multimedia tools throughout the book, I encourage you to consider the benefits of each type of multimedia and reflect on any other genres to which you might apply it in your classroom.

Now, if you're ready to learn more about how incorporating multimedia can reshape students' experiences writing in school, keep reading!

Section 1

Incorporating Multimedia into Argument Writing

1

Using Photos and Videos as Supporting Evidence

Let's begin our exploration of multimedia-enhanced writing by examining the use of photos and videos as supporting evidence in argument essays. We'll start with considering what this strategy is and then delve into why it can benefit students' argument writing. After that, we'll look at a description of a lesson on this concept and then examine some recommendations to keep in mind when helping your students use photos and videos as supporting evidence in their argument essays.

What Is It?

Authors of argument essays can incorporate photos and videos to accompany the text of their works; these multimedia should not take the place of an essay's text but rather provide authors with additional ways to convey information to their readers. I encourage students to take their own pictures and/or record their own videos when possible, as this allows them to get especially involved in researching their topic. However, even if a student is researching a topic that he or she can't directly photograph or record, that student can still enhance his or her work with photos and/or videos on the subject.

Let's start with an example of how this multimedia tool can look in action. I recently worked with a middle school student who was writing an essay about artwork displayed in public places. He supplemented his argument essay on the benefits of public artwork with photographs of public displays of art around his community. He included these images in his essay, along with captions that describe them. Figure 1.1 contains a

Figure 1.1 Student's Photograph of Public Art and Corresponding Caption

Here is an example of public art in Charlottesville, VA, where I live. This statue is on the side of a major highway. I think it's great because it's funny and people who are rushing to school and work can feel like they have something in common with it.

photograph this student took of public art in his town and a corresponding caption that he incorporated into his argument essay.

Why Is It Beneficial?

The use of photos and videos as supporting evidence can greatly benefit students' argument writing by allowing them to provide visual examples that supplement written explanations and helping them explore a topic in-depth. Let's take a look at each of these benefits separately.

Using Photos and Videos Helps Students
Supplement Written Explanations

The integration of photos and videos into argument writing allows students to reveal and illustrate ideas in ways that go beyond the written language in the text. For example, the photo of public art in Charlottesville,

Virginia, enables the author to show his readers what the artwork for which he's arguing can look like and allows them to see its benefits for themselves. This student commented on the importance of readers being able to see examples of the public art he discusses in his essay to understand what it is: "I think it really helps anyone reading the essay understand what I'm talking about. I describe the public art in my essay and talk about why I think it's important to have, but these examples make sure anyone reading understands what I'm talking about." In addition, this student author explained that incorporating multimedia in his essay visually reveals the benefits of public art to his readers: "Because of these photos [of examples of public art in the community], people can see on their own why [public art] is such a good thing. Sure, I still describe its positives and benefits in the essay, but these pictures let people reading also see the benefits on their own. I think that's really cool." It's important to note that, in both of these comments, this student emphasizes ways his multimedia support information in the text without taking its place. The images he includes provide important benefits but don't result in him incorporating fewer pieces of written information.

Using Photos and Videos Helps Students Explore Topics In-Depth

The integration of photos and videos into argument writing can also help authors and readers explore and understand topics in great detail. The author of the public-art essay felt that taking photos of art in his community and incorporating them into his piece resulted in him understanding his topic more than a traditional essay would: "I definitely think taking pictures of the public art in Charlottesville and using them in my essay helped me understand public art more than if this were just a regular essay—one with just writing and no pictures. Taking these pictures forced me to really get a close look at the public art and think about why it's a good thing. If I just wrote a normal paper, I would have still learned about this topic, but taking and including pictures helped me learn more."

It's important to note that incorporating this form of multimedia into argument writing can benefit students who take their own photos and videos as well as those who, because of the topics they're studying, can't photograph or record information themselves. I recently spoke with a student who wrote an argument essay about rainforest deforestation. Even though her topic required her to use photos and videos she found online instead of those she took personally, she still found that researching and incorporating multimedia helped her understand her topic very well: "Looking at pictures and videos of the destruction of rainforests—and then deciding which ones to put into my essay—definitely helped me understand deforestation. Deforestation was kind of a hard thing for me to picture when I began working on this essay, but looking at pictures and videos of it helped me get what it's like. I saw a video that showed a forest in Indonesia that was totally cleared out so people could put a plantation there. I really understood what deforestation's like after looking at that."

As these explanations and student insights reveal, the inclusion of photos and videos in argument writing can impact students in a number of positive ways, such as giving them opportunities to support written information in the text and helping them explore and understand their topics in great depth. In the next section, we'll take a look inside a middle school classroom and examine how I helped my eighth graders understand the effect that purposefully selected photos and videos can have on a piece of argument writing.

A Classroom Snapshot

"Today's a really important day," I begin class by informing my eighth graders. "We're going to take a big step toward you incorporating photos and videos into your argument essays. I'm very excited to share some ideas with you and hear your thoughts."

This is my third day talking with these students about including photos and videos in argument writing. In our first meeting, I introduced this strategy to the students and showed them an example of what an argument essay that uses photos and videos as supporting evidence can look like. Next, in our second class on the topic, we discussed why the incorporation of these multimedia can enhance a piece of argument writing. In today's class, I'll talk with the students about how to include photos and videos in their own argument essays.

"As you know," I remind the students, "we've been talking recently about using photos and videos in argument essays. Today, we'll be discussing how to think about incorporating these things in your own argument writing. I'm going to give you three recommendations to use when integrating photos and/or videos in your argument pieces. After I share each recommendation with you, I'm going to ask you to reflect on why you think it's important and how you can apply it to your own essay. Got it?"

Students around the room nod and verbally indicate agreement, so I continue: "The first recommendation I have for you is to make sure your photos and videos are directly related to the topic of your essay. Why do you think this is important to keep in mind?"

Student hands shoot up around the room; I call on a young lady who explains, "It's important because the photos and videos would be kind of pointless if they weren't [related to the essay's topic]."

"Yeah," interjects another student. "There wouldn't be much reason to include videos and photos that aren't about what the essay's about."

"Nicely said, both of you," I respond. "As you indicated, there's no real reason to include photos and videos that aren't related to your essay's topic. One on hand, this sounds fairly obvious: it's not like you would include pictures of dolphins in an argument essay about a topic that has nothing to do with dolphins, like whether the SAT should be required by colleges."

Students chuckle at this example, and I continue: "But there are times when people do incorporate photos and videos that aren't directly related to their topics. For example, imagine a student who is writing an argument essay about the danger of football players getting concussions. It's possible that a student might find any photo or video related to football, like a video of a quarterback throwing a ball or an image of a football stadium, for example, and say, 'This would be a good piece of multimedia to include in my essay.' In reality, though, it isn't directly related to the topic, because the topic is really about the danger of football-related concussions. What might be a better photo or video to include?"

A student raises his hand and replies, "One that's really related to concussions, like a photo or video of someone in a head-to-head collision."

"Absolutely right," I praise the student. "That's directly related to the topic we're discussing here. The examples I mentioned earlier of a video of a quarterback throwing a ball or an image of a stadium are related to football in general but aren't directly related to this topic. Does everyone see the difference?"

A chorus of agreement fills the classroom, and I continue to my next suggestion: "The second recommendation I'm going to share with you is related in some ways to the first. We just talked about making sure that the multimedia you incorporate in your essay should be related to the topic, but to make your work as strong as possible, I recommend making sure that the multimedia also focuses in on your most important points. I'll give you an example: Imagine you're writing an essay that argues in favor of teachers playing music in their classrooms. Let's say that one of your main points is that playing music in the classroom helps students focus on their work. Since that's one of your main points, it would really benefit your essay to include photos and/or videos that show students listening to music and being focused on their work, because those photos or videos would relate to the most important point in your essay. Now I have a follow-up question for you: How do you think you might apply this recommendation of making sure multimedia relates to an essay's most important points in your writing?"

To my delight, a number of student hands fly up around the room; I call on a student who shares her insights: "I can totally use this recommendation in my essay. My essay's about how we should start our school days later because teenagers are still waking up early in the morning when our school day starts. This is the main point of my essay, so I can use photos or videos of sleepy students in first period to emphasize this."

"That's a perfect example!" I praise the student's comment. "I love how you identified the main argument in your essay and thought about specific ways you could use multimedia to support it. When you all work on incorporating multimedia into your argument essays, I want you to first consider the main argument of your essay and then think about what kinds of photos and videos would best emphasize this main argument."

"There's one more recommendation for effectively incorporating multimedia that I want to share with you today," I continue. "When you include photos and videos in your argument essays, be sure that they help your readers visualize the topic you're describing. For example, if you're writing an argument essay about the impact of water pollution, you'll want to include photos and/or videos that help readers visualize the effect that water pollution can have on things like rivers, lakes, and wildlife. Now let's hear your thoughts: Why do you all think doing this can maximize the effectiveness of an argument essay?"

"Because," states a student, "it can make sure readers understand what you're arguing. Since they can see it, they can understand it even better."

"Plus," offers another, "it can help your argument by emphasizing whatever you're talking about. Like with what you said about water pollution: if you show readers pictures of some really polluted water, it can emphasize how bad water pollution really is."

"So well put!" I reply. "Using photos and videos that help readers visualize a topic can enhance readers' understanding and emphasize the point you're making. To summarize what we've discussed today: When you're thinking about incorporating photos and videos into your argument essays, make sure that the photos and videos you use relate to the topic of your essay, focus on your essay's most important points, and allow readers to clearly visualize the topic you're describing. All of these suggestions relate to the idea of using multimedia strategically—not just using it for the sake of doing so—in a way that really enhances your argument essay. In our next class, we'll work on selecting and incorporating photos and videos into our argumentative pieces. Great job today!"

Recommendations for Teaching Students about Using Photos and Videos as Supporting Evidence

In this section, I describe a step-by-step instructional process to use when teaching students about using photos and videos as supporting evidence in argument writing. The instructional steps I recommend are (1) show students examples of photos and videos that are used as supporting evidence in argument writing, (2) discuss with students how those photos and videos enhance the argument essays in which they are implemented, (3) give students suggestions for effectively incorporating multimedia in their argument essays, (4) work with students as they integrate photos and videos into their essays, and (5) ask students to reflect on how the multimedia they incorporated enhanced their works. Each of these recommendations is described in detail in this section.

1. Show students examples of photos and videos that are used as supporting evidence in argument writing.

This initial instructional recommendation is based on the idea of mentor texts—examples of effective writing that teachers show students to help them learn specific writing strategies and apply those tactics to their own works (Ehmann & Gayer, 2009). While this instructional tactic is most frequently associated with traditional writing strategies such as creating a strong lead or crafting sensory imagery, I suggest applying it to multimedia-enhanced writing as well. I introduce the idea of using photos and videos as supporting evidence for argument writing with my students by showing them a mentor example: a model that effectively uses multimedia for this purpose. On the first day I discussed this strategy with my students, I showed them an example of an argument essay I wrote about the importance of parents reading to children. In this essay, I describe the benefits of parents reading to their children and use photos and videos to support my argument. For example, when explaining that a benefit of parents reading to their children is that it exposes children to books above their

Figure 1.2 Image from My Argument Essay on Parents Reading to Their Children

grade level, I incorporate an image of me reading an above-grade-level book (C. S. Lewis's *The Lion, The Witch, and The Wardrobe*) to my eight-year-old son (as depicted in Figure 1.2). When working with your students, you can use this example, another from this book, or you can create your own example to share with your students (the most effective option!). Students are often more interested in writing when they see their teachers identifying as writers as well (Fletcher & Portalupi, 2001).

Once I've shown my students this image and the other multimedia I've used to support my argument, I'm ready to move to the next step of this instructional process.

2. Discuss with students how those photos and videos enhance the argument essays in which they are implemented.

Strong mentor text use goes beyond simply showing students examples of effective writing; it also involves discussing with students why certain writing strategies are important. After you've shown your students an example of an argument essay that incorporates multimedia, the next step is to talk with your students about why the photos and videos the author uses enhance the essay. I recommend helping your students transition to this more complex step by reviewing the multimedia in the argument essay you recently showed them and asking them to write down some ways they feel the use of multimedia enhances the piece. Once students have written down their thoughts, I suggest asking for volunteers to share their ideas with the rest of the class. While they do so, I record their responses on the whiteboard so that students can see each other's ideas. Once students have shared and explained their ideas, I add any other benefits I want them to note about how the use of multimedia in the piece strengthen it.

I recently conducted one of these discussions with my eighth graders; after showing them the photo depicted in Figure 1.2 that I included in my argument essay about parents reading to children, I asked them to reflect on how that image enhances the piece. One student explained that this image is especially beneficial because it depicts a young student listening to and following along to a high-level text: "I like how this picture shows you and your son reading a [difficult] book. The book y'all are reading—*The Lion, The Witch, and The Wardrobe*—uses big words and things like that, but your son is still getting to read it with you." Another student commented on the impact that this image has on the author's credibility: "It's cool that it's actually you reading a book to your son. You're not just telling people to read to kids; you're showing that you do it too. I think when someone actually does the thing they're telling others to do, it makes people believe them more." As these and other students shared their ideas about the impact of this image, I recorded their thoughts on the whiteboard. Once our discussion had concluded, I reviewed their comments and praised their insights: "You all did a very nice job of commenting on how this image enhances my argument essay on the importance of parents reading to children. Great work today!"

3. Give students suggestions for effectively incorporating multimedia in their argument essays.

This next step of the instructional process prepares students to take increased ownership of the inclusion of multimedia in argument writing, as it focuses on preparing them to strategically select the photos and videos they'd include in their own works. As described in this chapter's classroom snapshot, I give my students three key suggestions to keep in mind when determining which multimedia to incorporate into their argument essays:

◆ Make sure your photos and videos are directly related to the topic of your essay.
◆ Make sure that the multimedia you use highlights your most important points.
◆ Make sure that the multimedia you incorporate helps your readers visualize the topic you're describing.

After you share each of these recommendations with your students, I suggest asking them to reflect on why it is an important idea for argument writers to keep in mind. This gives students opportunities to consider the significance of these recommendations, which helps them further grasp the idea of carefully and strategically selecting multimedia to include in their works. Once students have shared their insights, extend their reflections even more by asking them how they might apply each of these recommendations to their own argument essays. This allows them to make specific connections to their own works, helping them consider particular forms of multimedia they'll incorporate into their argument essays and why they'll do so.

4. Work with students as they integrate photos and videos into their essays.

At this point the process, I recommend releasing even more responsibility to your students by asking them to select photos and videos to incorporate into their argument essays. Although students have more ownership at this stage, we teachers still need to support them as they integrate multimedia into their essays. To provide this support, I give each of my students a chart to use when evaluating whether or not

Figure 1.3 Analysis Questions for Integrating Multimedia

Summary of multimedia you are considering	
Is this multimedia directly related to the content of your essay?	
Does this multimedia highlight important information in your essay?	
Does this multimedia help readers visualize the topic of your essay?	

to include a particular form of multimedia in their works. This chart, depicted in Figure 1.3 and available in reproducible form in Appendix A, uses the suggestions discussed in the preceding recommendation to help students determine whether a specific photo or video can enhance a piece of argument writing. I tell my students that they should only incorporate multimedia for which they can answer "yes" to all three questions on this chart. When you confer with students who are incorporating videos, it's a good idea to check on the length of those videos and ensure their brevity. I encourage students to make sure their videos are no longer than five minutes; if the video is much longer than that, there's a much greater chance of the audience losing its focus.

I recently conferred with an eighth grader who was using this chart to determine which multimedia to incorporate in her argument essay about the importance of art class in middle school. She explained that she chose to include images of abstract paintings she and her classmates created. "I wrote 'yes' for all three questions," she shared. "I'm saying (in the essay) that art class is important because it's the only time in school when we get to use a certain kind of creativity. There are other kinds of creative thinking we do in school, but they're not like the kind of creative thinking we do in art class." The images of these abstract paintings, she stated, "are definitely directly related to the content of my essay, highlight important information, and absolutely help readers visualize the topic." Elaborating on these responses, she explained, "These paintings show the kind of creativity I'm talking about. They relate to my main point and help readers see what students can do in art class." This student's comments show that she had thought carefully about the alignment of this form of multimedia and the piece's topic; her insightful responses indicate that she clearly understands what she wants to get across to readers and how these images will help convey that message.

5. Ask students to reflect on how the multimedia they incorporated enhanced their works.

This final step of the instructional process facilitates student metacognition by asking them to reflect on how the multimedia they included in their argument essays improved their works. I recommend helping students consider the importance of these multimedia by presenting them with two related reflection questions:

- How did the multimedia you incorporated into your argument essay enhance your piece?
- What would your argument essay be missing without the multimedia you incorporated?

I suggest asking students to first respond to these questions in their notebooks, then share their thoughts with partners, and finally inform the rest of the class of their ideas. This structure gives students time to consider these questions and process their thoughts before contributing them to a whole-class discussion.

The student mentioned previously who incorporated photos of student artwork into an essay about the importance of art classes in school responded to the first of these questions by saying, "The images of abstract art I included enhance my piece by letting readers see an example of the kind of creativity students use in art class and showing them that this is a different kind of creativity than they use in other parts of school." In response to the second question, she commented, "If I didn't use these images, my essay wouldn't give such a clear example of the kind of creativity I'm talking about in the essay."

Final Thoughts on Using Photos and Videos as Supporting Evidence

- Authors of argument essays can incorporate photos and videos to accompany the text of their works.
- These multimedia should not take the place of an essay's text but rather provide authors with additional ways to convey information to their readers.
- The use of photos and videos as supporting evidence can greatly benefit students' argument writing in two key ways:
  - They help students supplement written explanations.
  - They help students explore topics in depth.
- Use the following steps when teaching students about using photos and videos as supporting evidence in argument writing:
  - Show students examples of photos and videos that are used as supporting evidence in argument writing.
  - Discuss with students how those photos and videos enhance the argument essays in which they are implemented.

◆ Give students suggestions for effectively incorporating multimedia in their argument essays.

◆ Work with students as they integrate photos and videos into their essays.

◆ Ask students to reflect on how the multimedia they incorporated enhanced their works.

2

Connecting to Authentic Audiences through Student-Created Websites

In this chapter, we'll examine how student-created websites can play an important role in argument writing instruction by helping students connect with others who share their interests. First, we'll look at what this concept is, exploring its fundamental features and an example of a student's work. Then, we'll explore the benefits of using student-created websites in writing instruction. Next, we'll check out a description of a lesson on this topic; finally, we'll conclude by examining some recommendations to use when you help your students create websites that help them share their ideas with authentic audiences.

What Is It?

In this form of multimedia use, students create websites that allow them to share their argument essays and other related information with interested individuals. I ask my students to include the following information on their websites: a "welcome page" that clearly communicates the topic to viewers, a description of why the student is interested in the topic, a link to the text of the argument essay the student created, and a list of recommended resources readers can examine if they are interested in learning more. I also encourage students to include a way for readers to provide feedback on their work and ask questions. All of these features can be incorporated into the websites without students including their names; I leave the inclusion of students' names on these websites up to them and their families.

Now, let's take a look at an example of a student-created website that can facilitate connections with authentic audiences. Recall how, in

Figure 2.1 Home Page of Website on the Importance of Public Art in Charlottesville, Virginia

THE IMPORTANCE OF PUBLIC ART IN CHARLOTTESVILLE, VA

This site is about the importance of public art in my hometown of Charlottesville. I am very interested in this topic because I think the public art in Charlottesville helps make the city beautiful and unique. The pages on this site contain an argument essay I wrote about the why I think the public art in Charlottesville is important, information about why I'm interested in it, other articles about public art, and a form to contact me and discuss the importance of public art.

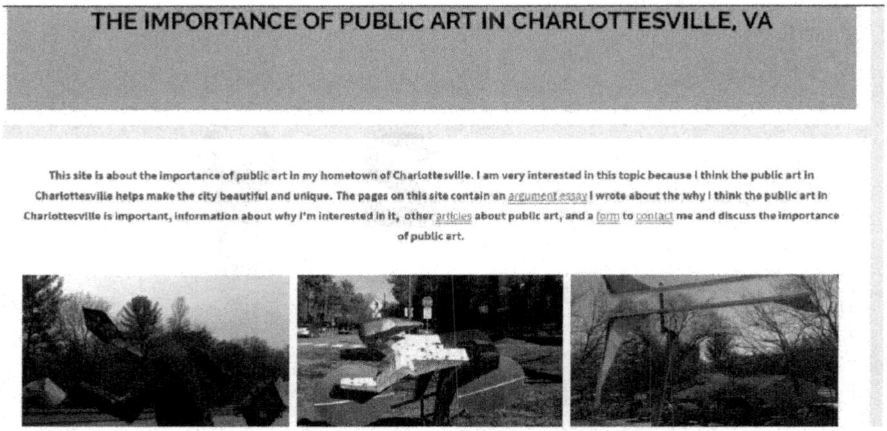

Chapter One, we looked at an example of student work that incorporated an image of public art in the student's community; this student also created a website about the significance of public art in his town. On this site, he included his essay on the topic, information about why he is interested in it, some links to other articles about public art, a form for interested individuals to contact him, and a home page that introduces viewers to the topic and contains links to the other information on the site. Figure 2.1 depicts the home page of this student's website on the importance of public art in Charlottesville, Virginia.

Now that we've considered what a student-created website on an argument writing topic can look like, let's examine how this multimedia use can benefit students.

Why Is It Beneficial?

The major benefit of students creating websites on argument writing topics is that it allows them to communicate their ideas with broader audiences than just their teachers—a feature that is associated with a number of positive outcomes. One of these positive outcomes is that students who write for authentic audiences are often more motivated than those who produce works that are only read by their teachers (Fletcher & Portalupi, 2001). Even though literacy is often viewed as an individualistic endeavor in which students read and write by themselves and communicate their ideas to their teachers, the reality is that reading and writing are most effective when viewed as communal activities, where students are able to share their areas of interest and expertise with their peers, especially those that enjoy similar things (Knoester, 2009).

My work in the classroom reflects these research findings; the student who created the webpage on public art in his hometown loved the opportunity to share his ideas with others who possess similar interests: "My favorite part of doing this was putting my ideas on a website so other people could read them and then actually getting some comments from people who agreed with me. After I finished the website, I texted the link to other people I know that I thought would also be interested and they wrote me back with a lot of nice compliments. That was very cool and exciting." This student's comments reveal the enjoyment he derived from getting positive feedback on his work, a benefit facilitated by sharing his ideas on a website. Another student who shared her argument essay on a website she created expressed a similar idea, explaining that she "thought it was really awesome that other people could read" her work, sharing that this possibility "gave [her] extra motivation to do a great job."

Another positive result of students sharing their works with authentic audiences is that it requires them to think carefully about the piece's potential readers (Fletcher & Portalupi, 2001). When students write papers that will only be read by their teachers, they are writing for a specific, known reader. Students typically assume that this reader has a solid background understanding of the topic and sometimes even know exactly what she or he knows about it. However, writing for a more wide-ranging audience produces a different experience: since students don't know exactly who will read the piece and what kind of prior knowledge those readers have, they must think about possible questions readers might have about the topic and information readers need to know in order to understand it as well as possible. For example, the student who created the public art website explained that he thought differently about this website, knowing that it would be read by more people than just his teacher: "If [my teacher] was the only one reading this, I don't think I would have needed to think about it as much because I know that she knows about the artwork I'm talking about, where exactly it is in town, and other things like that. Since some people looking at my website and the information on it might not know those things, I had to be sure to put information like that and other things they'd need to know about in my website." This comment illustrates the critical thinking associated with writing for a general, unknown audience; this student anticipated the audience's potential questions and addressed them when determining what information to include on his site.

There are several possible ways to maximize the potential audience of students' websites: students can share the sites themselves through social media and personal communication (such as the previously described student who texted the link to his site to others he thought might be interested), schools can share the links on their websites and in their newsletters, and students can post the links to online communities for others interested in a similar topic (for example, a student who created a website arguing in favor of changing certain rules in baseball could post a link to the site on an online message board read by other baseball enthusiasts).

So, why can sharing their works with authentic audiences benefit students? As the research and examples in this section illustrate, this practice can both motivate students and require them to think carefully about their audience's potential questions. In the next section, we'll take a look inside a seventh-grade classroom and examine my discussion with my students on this topic.

A Classroom Snapshot

"You all did such great work yesterday," I begin today's lesson with my seventh graders, "and I can't wait to see what you come up with today, when we build off the ideas I introduced in yesterday's class."

These students and I are in our second day of discussing the idea of connecting with authentic audiences in argument writing through student-created websites. In our first class, I introduced this multimedia use to the students, talking with them about what one should include in this kind of website and showing them an example of such a site. I created this example as a model to show them; it focuses on the importance of parents reading to their children, incorporating a home page that introduces the topic and contains links to the site's other pages. On these pages, readers can find my argument essay, a description of why I'm interested in the topic, a form for readers to use to contact me, and related articles on this topic.

In today's class, I will lead the students in a discussion about why websites such as this one are effective ways of sharing arguments with audiences. We'll begin by specifically analyzing this site and then think in more "big picture" terms about the benefits of using multimedia in this way. After reviewing highlights of the previous day's conversation with the students, I introduce the day's focus: "Today, we're going to talk about why the website I introduced to you yesterday is an effective way of sharing an argument. The goal for this discussion is for you all to understand why it can be a good idea to use websites to share ideas that you might want to argue about. This way, you can keep those reasons in mind later on when you create your own websites that you'll use to share your arguments."

I pause, looking around at the students, pleased that they all appear engaged and ready to dive into today's activity. I continue, "Let's get started by taking another look at the website I introduced to you in our last class; as I hope you remember, this is a site I created about the importance of parents reading to their children." I project an image of this website on the screen in front of the classroom. Figure 2.2 depicts the home page of the site. (A link to it is available in Appendix C.)

The students and I review the contents of this site, starting with its home page and then looking at the rest of its material. Once we've looked at this information, I introduce the next step of our activity: "Now, I'm going to ask you all to work in groups to answer this question: Why is

Figure 2.2 Home Page of Website on the Importance of Parents Reading to Children

creating a website like this one an effective way to share an argument? I'll come around and check in with each group as you discuss these ideas."

I begin to circulate the room and check in with the students, first sitting down with a group that is having a spirited conversation. "I love how excited about this you all are," I share, smiling. "Talk to me what you're discussing."

A particularly animated student speaks first: "I was just saying how cool I think it is that making websites helps you share your ideas with people. You can make a site and put it up on Facebook or Twitter, which is really cool, I think."

"And," interjects another student, "you might get to share your ideas with all kinds of people. You can share your site with people you know, but there's also a chance that it can get read by other people—people you don't know. I think that's cool, too, because you get to share your ideas with so many different people."

"These are very insightful comments," I respond. "I love how you noticed a lot of benefits that can come from being able to share your ideas with others. I agree with you that this is an excellent benefit of creating a site like this one. Keep talking about any other benefits you can think of. Great job so far!"

The students in this group smile at my comments, and I continue to move around the room. I sit down with the next group I come to and ask them about their conversation so far: "What do you all think? Why might creating a website like the one we looked at be an effective way to share an argument?"

"I think it's because you can use so much technology to get your point across," responds a student in the group.

"That's a very interesting point," I respond. "Tell me more."

"Well," explains another student in the group, "we talked about how we think it's awesome that a website lets you use more than just the words in an essay to make your message come through. Like, you get to use pictures on your website and you can use graphics and things like that make the website with a good-looking format that will get people interested and make them want to read more."

"Nicely said," I tell the student. "You're really noticing the benefits of using this form of technology. That's important because it shows that you understand why creating a website can be useful for this specific purpose. When you understand the benefits of using a specific form of technology, it shows that you're using that type of technology because it's the most effective way of doing something, not just because you want to use some technology. Excellent job, you all."

I continue around the room, visiting and talking with the other small groups. Once I've met with each group, I address the class: "You all did a great job today. I'm so impressed by your thoughtful comments about why creating a website is an effective way to share an argument. Some groups talked about how websites help you share your ideas with others, others talked about the benefits of the technological features websites provide, and others talked about a combination of these things. We're out of time for today, but we'll begin next class with each group sharing its specific insights on this topic. Then we'll discuss specific suggestions for you to keep in mind when creating your own sites to share your arguments!"

Recommendations for Teaching Students about Connecting to Authentic Audiences through Student-Created Websites

In this section, I describe a step-by-step process for teaching students about connecting to authentic audiences through student-created websites. I recommend that teachers follow five key steps: (1) show students examples of websites that share arguments, (2) discuss with students why these websites are effective ways of sharing arguments, (3) give students suggestions for crafting their own websites that share arguments with authentic audiences, (4) work with students as they create their own websites for this purpose, and (5) ask students to reflect on the benefits of creating websites to share their arguments. These recommendations are discussed in detail in this section.

1. Show students examples of websites that share arguments.

This opening activity gives students an introduction to what they'll ultimately be creating by showing them what an argument-sharing website looks like and introducing them to such a site's key features. When I present to students an example of a website that shares an argument, I like to show them one that I made myself. This often helps them see that the creation of a site like this is an attainable goal and allows me to answer specific questions about website creation they have. The website I show my students—and the one I've referred to in this chapter—focuses on the importance of parents reading to their children. When I share this site, I identify its key features, such as its welcome page that orients viewers, the tabs on the top of the page that identify the other information included in the site, and the resources and ideas included on each of these pages.

I recommend creating your own website to show students what an argument-sharing site looks like. Many website-building programs provide free templates that are attractive and easy to use. Make sure that your site contains the same types of information you want your students' versions to include; for example, I created a site containing a welcome page, a description of why I'm interested in the topic, an argument essay I wrote, a form to use for contacting me, and links to additional resources on the topic. In addition to sharing the site you construct, you can also show your students the argument-focused website I created, which can be found at http://readtochildren.weebly.com. (This link is also available in Appendix C.)

The feedback I've received from students about this activity indicates that they really appreciate seeing an example of an argument-sharing website before being asked to create one on their own. One young lady explained, "I really liked that we started by looking at a website you made. If you would have just said, 'Go make a website,' that would have been, like, really stressful, but you showed us an example of what to do. That made it much easier."

2. Discuss with students why these websites are effective ways of sharing arguments.

This step of the instructional process builds off of the first one: while the initial step introduced students to examples to argument-sharing websites, this follow-up helps students consider what makes these sites especially effective. As described in this chapter's classroom snapshot, I begin these discussions by stating the lesson's goal, explaining that the day's objective is for students to reflect on the benefits of using a website to share an argument. Next, I review the features of the website I showed the students in the previous class. Following this, I often ask the students to work in groups to reflect on why creating a website like the example I showed them is an effective way to share an argument.

While the students work, I recommend circulating the room and checking on each group's progress. Recall from the classroom snapshot that one group I met with focused on how websites help argument essay authors share their ideas with others, while another group discussed the ways websites' technology features help authors convey their points. Different groups will often identify distinct benefits of these websites based on the ideas and interests of their members. I try to validate each group's observations and highlight aspects of their insights that are particularly relevant. Once you've checked in with all of the groups, it can be beneficial to ask each group to share its ideas with the rest of the class. This allows each group to comment on the benefits of this multimedia tool and helps the rest of students learn from all the different perspectives in the class.

3. Give students suggestions for crafting their own websites that share arguments with authentic audiences.

Now that students have examined an example of an argument-sharing website and reflected on its benefits, it's time to help them start thinking about suggestions for crafting their own sites that share arguments with authentic audiences. When preparing my students to create their own sites, I give them three key recommendations: (1) consider ways to make your website visually engaging, (2) ensure that your site illustrates your beliefs about its topic, and (3) make sure your website conveys why this topic is important to you. I introduce these suggestions to my students, ask them to reflect on why each one is important, and then talk with them about how to put each of these recommendations into action when crafting their sites.

The first of these suggestions, which calls for students to consider ways to make their sites visually engaging, encourages them to capitalize on the benefits of this form of multimedia. When I asked my students to reflect on this recommendation, a number of them commented on the opportunities websites provide for crafting a visually attractive resource and how an aesthetically pleasing site can engage readers. One student remarked on the "whole bunch of options and designs" that many website templates provide, explaining, "You can use a lot of different color combinations, fonts, and borders, so you can try different things and see what looks best." He continued to assert that when one makes a "good-looking website, people are going to spend more time with and read what you have to say." Another student noted how websites allow their creators to "use photos and videos, like the ones we used in our argument essays." This student explained that these images and videos "are awesome because they make [the website] look good and are related to [the author's] point."

The second recommendation reminds students to ensure their sites illustrate their beliefs about their topics. While it may seem self-explanatory that an argument-sharing website conveys a stance on a topic, some student websites do not do this. I've worked with students who crafted websites that nicely introduced a topic but didn't actually assert the author's stance. This issue relates to a similar occurrence in students' argument writing: when researching my book *The Argument Writing Toolkit* (Ruday, 2015), I noticed that students sometimes created introductory paragraphs that described the overall issue about which they were arguing but didn't actually take a stance on that issue. Just as this can happen in the students' essays, it has the potential to occur on their websites as well. I tell my students that someone should look at the "welcome" page of their websites (the first part of the site that viewers encounter) and immediately be able to answer the question: "What does the creator of this site believe about this topic?" If a site's readers can't quickly answer that question, the creator should revise the site to accentuate that information.

The third suggestion I give my students to keep in mind while they create their sites is to make sure the website conveys why the topic is important to them. I recently explained this recommendation to a group of students by saying, "A really strong argument website does more than use visuals well and conveys its argument clearly. It also shows the author's passion for the topic." I continued to explain this idea by referring to specific aspects of my site on the importance of parents reading to children: "On my site, I describe my interest in parents reading to their children briefly on the welcome page and then discuss it in more detail on the page titled 'Why I'm Interested.' The information I give in these parts of the website helps anyone looking at it understand why the topic is important to me." After pointing out these features, I asked my students why they think this a significant part of an effective argument-sharing website. One student explained, "I think it's really important to show that you're interested in whatever your website's about. That makes [the website] a lot more interesting." Another student concurred, "Yeah, I want to read something a lot more if the author shows that they're interested."

4. Work with students as they create their own websites for this purpose.

At this point in the instructional process, the students should be ready to craft their own argument-sharing websites. I recommend asking the students to work independently on this task and checking in with them as they do so. When I meet with students, I look to see if they're applying the three recommendations described in the previous suggestion; following these suggestions can maximize the effectiveness of their sites. To guide the students as they work and facilitate my conversations with them, I give them the chart depicted in Figure 2.3 and available in reproducible form in Appendix A. This chart asks students to reflect on whether they've incorporated each of the three recommendations and to cite specific evidence from their sites of having done so.

Figure 2.3 Guideline Chart for Creating Websites

Guideline Question	Your Response	Evidence That Supports Your Response
Does your website contain features that make it visually engaging?		
Does your site state your beliefs about its topic?		
Does your site convey why its topic is important to you?		

While recently meeting with students about the websites they were creating, I spoke with a young lady who was crafting a site related to her argument that her school should offer more girls' sports teams:

"Tell me about your work on your site so far," I began.

"It's going great!" she replied. "I've definitely got things here that make it visually strong. I found a great sports-themed template online and I have pictures of girls playing a whole bunch of sports to really show that it's good to give girls a lot of options for which sports they want to play."

"Nice job," I responded. "I love how specific you were in identifying ways you've made the site visually engaging. The next thing on the guideline chart is a question that asks if your site states your beliefs about the topic. Do you feel yours does that?"

"Oh, yeah, absolutely," she answered. "The title of my website is 'Girls Need More Sports Options.' And, in the part on the first page where I introduce readers to my site, I say that I made this site to convince others that girls need more sports options at our school. I also have my argument essay on the site, so that's another way it shows my beliefs."

"Wonderful! Now," I continued, "the last question on this chart is whether this site conveys why its topic is important to you. What do you think about your site in relation to that question?"

"My site definitely shows the importance of this topic to me. I say on the first page that this topic matters to me because I feel like my sports options are limited at [my school] and that boys here have a bunch more options. I also put a specific page on the site that's just about why this topic is important to me. I give even more reasons on that one."

Once you've met with your students and heard their thoughts on the sites they're creating, you'll be ready to move to the final step of this instructional process, in which students reflect on the benefits of creating websites to share their arguments.

5. Ask students to reflect on the benefits of creating websites to share their arguments.

This final step of the instructional process emphasizes the importance of reflection, calling for students to consider the benefits of the websites they created to share their arguments. While other steps in this process also ask students to think of the benefits of creating websites to share arguments, this one is different because it focuses specifically on the students' experiences creating their own sites, not on their analyses of other sites. To help students reflect on the benefits of creating their own argument-sharing websites, I ask them to respond to the question, "What are some ways your website helped you share your argument as effectively as possible?"

I recommend asking students to first respond to this question in writing, then tell their answers to a partner, and finally volunteer to share their thoughts with the whole class. This sequence of events gives them time to process their ideas and opportunities to share them in low-stakes ways before doing so with the whole class. One seventh-grade student with whom I recently worked explained that the various features of the website encouraged him to think carefully about how he was presenting his argument: "Making a website really made me think more about my argument because I had to do more than just write an essay. I had to include so many different things, like pictures, a website format, and a description of why I'm interested. Doing all that made me think about my topic a lot more than just doing an essay would." This student's comments are especially significant because they not only reveal his awareness of the features of his site, but also how those features impacted his experience thinking about and presenting his argument. Another student noted that she was motivated by the idea that her site was to be read by a wider audience than her normal work was: "I think it put extra effort into this because I knew my friends and a lot of other people would read it. That totally motivated me to do good work."

Final Thoughts on Connecting to Authentic Audiences through Student-Created Websites

- ◆ In this form of multimedia use, students create websites that allow them to share their argument essays and other related information with interested individuals.
- ◆ I ask my students to include the following information on their websites:
  - ◆ A "welcome page" that clearly communicates the topic to viewers

- ◆ A description of why the student is interested in the topic
- ◆ A link to the text of the argument essay the student created
- ◆ A list of recommended resources readers can examine if they are interested in learning more
- ◆ The major benefit of students creating websites on argument writing topics is that it allows them to communicate their ideas with broader audiences than just their teachers—a feature that is associated with a number of positive outcomes.
  - ◆ One of these positive outcomes is that students who write for authentic audiences are often more motivated than those that produce works that are only read by their teachers.
  - ◆ Another positive result of students sharing their works with authentic audiences is that it requires them to think carefully about the piece's potential readers (Fletcher & Portalupi, 2001).
- ◆ When teaching students about connecting to authentic audiences through student-created websites,
  - ◆ Show students examples of websites that share arguments.
  - ◆ Discuss with students why these websites are effective ways of sharing arguments.
  - ◆ Give students suggestions for crafting their own websites that share arguments with authentic audiences.
  - ◆ Work with students as they create their own websites for this purpose.
  - ◆ Ask students to reflect on the benefits of creating websites to share their arguments.

Section 2

Incorporating Multimedia into Informational Writing

3

Creating Video Topic Trailers

Let's turn our attention to ways that multimedia can enhance informational writing instruction, starting with an exploration of how students can create video topic trailers about their informational writing topics. We'll begin by considering what it means to create video topic trailers and then consider how doing so can enhance students' experiences with informational writing. Next, we'll look at an example of a lesson on this argument writing strategy; finally, we'll conclude by considering five key recommendations to keep in mind when helping your students create their own video topic trailers.

What Is It?

A video topic trailer is a short film that a student creates about an informational writing topic; this trailer should accompany the student's informational essay and provide a short introduction to the piece's topic. Instead of providing a comprehensive overview of all the information the essay addresses, the topic trailer provides a kind of preview that conveys selected, high-interest details about the essay's subject and piques readers' curiosity levels enough for them to want to learn more. Since the goal of these topic trailers is to introduce the topic and get readers interested, they should be relatively brief: I recommend asking students to keep theirs between two and five minutes. (The example you'll see in this chapter is just under three minutes long.) These videos can be created using fairly basic technological equipment—advanced devices and knowledge levels are definitely not needed! My students typically record their topic trailers on their (or their parents') cell phones using the video recording feature;

I discourage them from using high-level video editing programs because I want the focus to be primarily on their ideas, not on special effects.

I recently worked with a student who created a video topic trailer to introduce his informational essay on hybrid cars. This video began with the student standing in front of his family's Toyota Prius and explaining that his video trailer and corresponding essay are about the features of hybrid cars. As the video progressed, the student also identified key features inside the car and explained those features' importance. This video was about two and a half minutes long and gave a fun and engaging introduction to the student's informational writing topic of hybrid cars.

While this student was able to feature an example of his topic in his video, this is not always possible. For example, another student with whom I recently worked wrote an informational essay on the U.S. Women's World Cup Soccer Team. Since she did not have access to the actual players on the team, this student improvised; her video began with a recording of her on a soccer field, in which she demonstrated a few soccer moves and talked about how the U.S. Women's World Cup Team inspired her to play the game. Then, she held up images of important players on the U.S. Team, such as Mia Hamm and Alex Morgan, and explained their contributions to the team. The end result was an engaging video that nicely introduced readers to her essay's topic.

As these examples illustrate, video topic trailers can vary somewhat but should all introduce the informational essay's subject in a brief, engaging way, providing viewers with some key information about the subject. In the next section, we'll consider why creating video topic trailers can be important to effective informational writing.

Why Is It Beneficial?

Creating video topic trailers for informational essays has a number of potential benefits; this activity requires students to identify key information in their works, reflect on how to use video to engage potential readers, and interact with their topics in unique ways. In this section, we'll explore each of these benefits.

Students Identify Key Information

Students who create video topic trailers are required to think carefully about their topic and identify key information they would like to share with potential readers. I tell my students that a topic trailer shouldn't provide a comprehensive list of every fact and detail about a certain concept; instead, it should provide a few facts that they feel are especially significant. For example, when my student who worked on the topic of hybrid cars was planning his trailer, I encouraged him to look through all the facts he included in his essay and identify two or three that he thought would be most informative and interesting to someone learning about the topic. He chose to describe key features of hybrid cars that allow them to be so fuel efficient, such as their power sources and design. This process of considering a number of facts and deciding which ones to include in a topic trailer requires students to think critically about information; instead of reading all the facts they've accumulated about a topic, the identification of key information requires students to analyze the information they've learned and determine which details would be most beneficial to their audience and why.

Students Reflect on How to Use Video to Engage Potential Readers

When students create video topic trailers, they must reflect on the best ways to use the video features of those trailers to engage potential readers. This idea extends logically from the previous one—just as students need to identify the facts that will be most useful and intriguing to their potential readers, they also have to consider how they will shoot and structure their videos in ways that will best keep readers interested in learning more about the topic. Reflecting on the most engaging and informative ways to structure their videos requires them to think analytically about what makes a topic trailer effective and why; this activity calls for students to engage in metacognitive reflection about the strongest ways to inform and engage an audience, taking the critical choices they must make as writers and applying them to a new medium.

Both of the previously described students thought carefully about how to craft their videos. The student who made a topic trailer about hybrid cars explained his process as follows: "I wanted to begin the video with me in front of the car because I thought that would be a good way to introduce the kind of car I was talking about. Then, I showed specific things about the car to give more specifics to people watching the video." Similarly, the student who recorded a trailer about the U.S. Women's World Cup Soccer Team commented on the ideas that went into her video: "I thought a lot about how to make [the topic trailer]. I wanted to talk about players that have been on the team, like Alex [Morgan] and Mia [Hamm], but I also wanted to have some kind of introduction, so I introduced the topic first with me playing soccer and explaining what the topic was and then went into talking about important players on the team." These students' comments reveal their thoughtful analysis of the most effective ways to construct the video trailers they created.

Students Interact with Their Topics in Unique Ways

Video topic trailers can also benefit student writers by giving them an opportunity to interact with their topic in unique ways; the process of conceptualizing and recording one of these trailers calls for students to go beyond the typical informational writing procedures of researching a topic and writing about it. While students who create trailers still engage in research and writing, they also must think creatively about how to best convey information about their topic on video. Students with whom I've worked have asserted that the uniqueness of creating video topic trailers is both challenging and enjoyable; the individual who created the video about the U.S. Women's World Cup Team expressed both of these ideas: "Doing this was really hard! At first, it sounds easy: 'You're gonna make a short video about your topic.' But it was actually hard because you had to think about what kind of information you were going to include and then how to make a video that makes your topic interesting to readers. . . Even though it was hard, it was also really fun, too! I've never made a video for school before, and I really enjoyed it. I got to show off my soccer skills and also describe my topic in a different way than just writing about it."

As these examples and explanations illustrate, video topic trailers provide a new dimension to informational writing. Asking students to identify key information, reflect on ways to engage readers, and interact with material in unique ways requires them to look at informational writing differently than they otherwise would. In the next section, we'll take a look inside a sixth-grade classroom and examine how my students and I discuss ideas for creating video topic trailers.

A Classroom Snapshot

"You all are almost ready to use the force," I smilingly tell my students at the beginning of class. "You have learned much so far, but you still have some more to learn."

After my students laugh, I clarify: "Of course, when I say 'use the force,' I'm talking about creating one of the video topic trailers that we've been discussing. In today's class, we're going to talk about some important suggestions to keep in mind when creating your video topic trailers. I'm going to give you three suggestions that I think are especially significant. After I share each one with you, I'm going to ask you for your thoughts on why you think that suggestion could be important to creating a strong video topic trailer on an informational writing topic."

Today is our third class session on creating video topic trailers that align with students' informational writings. (These students have already written informational essays and are now exploring how to craft video topic trailers to introduce them.) First, we looked at examples of video topic trailers and discussed the features they possess. Then, in our second class on this multimedia tool, the students and I worked together to analyze how video topic trailers can enhance a piece of informational writing. Today's class marks a conceptual shift in our examination of this concept, as our conversation will move away from discussing existing examples and toward students creating their trailers.

I begin this discussion by introducing the first suggestion for creating a video topic trailer: "The first tip I have for you all is to select some especially significant facts that you'll share in your video topic trailer. To do this, I suggest first looking through your informational writings and highlighting the facts you incorporated about your topic. Once you've done that, make a list of the two or three facts that you think would be most interesting and informative to someone who's learning about your topic: these are the facts that you'll want to be sure you include in your topic trailer."

After sharing these ideas with the students, I ask them for their insights: "What do you all think about this? Why might it be important to select some especially significant facts about your topic to include in your video topic trailer?"

"I think," answers a student, "that it's important because you don't want to just give a whole long list of facts. People will stop listening if you do that. It's better to just do a few facts because that will probably get people to listen better and more closely."

"And," interjects another student, "it's good to make sure you pick the most important facts. If you only pick a couple things to say, you want to make sure those things are really important things."

"Very nicely said, both of you," I reply. "You both did great work identifying reasons why it's important to pick out significant facts to include in video topic trailers."

"Now," I continue, "the second suggestion I have for you all as you create your video topic trailers is to plan the visual images you'll display in your video. Before you start recording your video, you'll want to plan out exactly what the viewer will see in each part of it. I recommend making a storyboard—a visual sequence of what viewers will see throughout the video. To make the storyboard, I suggest taking a piece of paper and drawing four squares of equal size on it. Then, draw four scenes that you envision taking place in your video topic trailer."

Students around the classroom nod, appearing engaged in this idea, and I explain further: "Let's think of an example of how this can look. Remember the example trailer we looked at together—the one where a boy discussed the features of hybrid cars? That student planned out his video with a four-scene storyboard. In his first square, he drew an image of himself in front of the Toyota Prius we saw in the video. In the second square, he drew the car's streamlined front and low-to-the ground build to show that he'd be focusing on that feature next. Then, in the third square, he drew the car's engine to show that he was going to talk about the engines of hybrid cars. Finally, in the fourth one, he sketched a picture of the car's dashboard to show that he was going to finish by talking about the car's dashboard display and how it relates to the features of hybrid cars."

"Now that I've introduced this suggestion," I tell the students, "and discussed this example, I'm very interested to hear what you think: Why might it be a good idea to plan the events of your video topic trailer on a storyboard?"

I am thrilled by the large number of students who volunteer to share their ideas. "It's a good idea because it makes you have a plan before you start," asserts one student. "If you didn't put the events on the storyboard, you might just get started without a plan, and then your video wouldn't be organized."

"That's an excellent point," I reply. "Putting the events on the story-board ensures that you'll have a plan for your video topic trailer before you start recording it. Nicely said. Can anyone think of another benefit of using a storyboard to plan?"

A student raises her hand and explains, "It helps you see exactly how things will look, like where you'll stand and what things you'll show or do in your video. I'm doing mine on the animals in my family's farm, and I think using a storyboard will help me see how things will look in my video before I make it."

"Wonderful," I respond. "That's a really insightful idea and a great example to go with it."

"Next," I continue, "we're going to think about the final suggestion I have for you when planning your video topic trailers: in addition to select-ing especially important facts and using a storyboard to plan out your video, I recommend that you come up with a strong opening statement that you'll deliver in your video. At the beginning of the topic trailer, you'll want to have an opening statement that clearly communicates what your video is about and gets the viewer's attention. For example, I've told some of you that I love running and have run the Boston Marathon. I would begin a trailer about the Boston Marathon by saying the following: 'Have you ever ran a race? If you're like most people, you probably have. Today, I'm going to talk to you about a very special race: the Boston Marathon, which is the oldest and most famous road race in the United States.' The very beginning of this statement is designed to get the audience's attention by asking the people who are watching the video if they've ever ran a race. My hope is that this question gets them interested and wanting to know more about why I'm asking this. Then, I begin to introduce the specific topic of the trailer by informing viewers that I'll be telling them about the Boston Marathon."

"What do you all think?" I ask the students. "Why do think it could be important to have an opening statement in your topic trailer that clearly communicates what your video is about and gets the viewer's attention?"

To my delight, student hands fly up around the room. A number of students reply; all of their responses resemble the comment shared by a student who explained, "Doing this gets the people watching your video interested and makes sure they know what it's about. These are both important things to do, so you definitely want to make sure you do both of them. You want people watching to be interested and you want them to know what's going on."

Recommendations for Teaching Students about Creating Video Topic Trailers

In this section, I describe a step-by-step instructional process to use when teaching students about creating video topic trailers related to their informational writings. The instructional steps I recommend are (1) show students examples of video topic trailers that introduce informational writing topics, (2) talk with students about how video topic trailers can enhance an audience's experience, (3) give students suggestions for creating their own video topic trailers, (4) work with students as they plan their own video topic trailers, and (5) ask students to reflect on the beneficial components of the video topic trailers they created. Each of these recommendations is discussed in detail in this section.

1. Show students examples of video topic trailers that introduce informational writing topics.

Beginning this instructional process by showing students examples of video topic trailers provides them with clear examples and an understanding of what they'll ultimately be producing. You can do this by showing your students the example provided in this chapter of a student-created topic trailer about hybrid cars, which can be accessed at https://www.youtube.com/watch?v=yaC9FcSD7H4. (This link is also included in Appendix C.) This model gives students an understanding of what a video topic trailer can look like and the kind of information that might be included in one. Another excellent option is to create your own trailer about a topic that would be engaging to your students; this allows you as a teacher to align the topic and structure with your students' particular interests and skills. Whether you use an existing topic trailer, one that you create, or both, what's most important is that you're giving your students a concrete example to follow when they craft their own video topic trailers. Several of the elementary and middle school students I've taught have commented on how much viewing these examples has helped them; one sixth grader indicated, "Thank you so much for showing us what this looked like! That really helped me know what to do!"

2. Talk with students about how video topic trailers can enhance an audience's experience.

I like to begin this stage of the instructional process by emphasizing the importance of using multimedia purposefully; in a recent conversation with students on this topic, I explained, "Now that we've seen what a video topic trailer can look like, we're going to think about how creating them can benefit your audience. After all, there wouldn't be any reason to make video topic trailers if they didn't benefit your audience in some way." I then identify two key ways video topic trailers can enhance an audience's experience: they engage viewers in the piece's topic and introduce audiences to important facts about that topic.

After identifying these benefits of video topic trailers, I like to explain to students why each one can enhance the audience's experience. When addressing the first idea, that topic trailers engage viewers in the piece's topic, I focus on the multi-sensory aspects and relatively short duration of video topic trailers, emphasizing that these trailers have the potential to grab an audience's attention and get them interested in a topic in a way a written text might not: "A piece of writing can be really interesting, but it might not immediately engage a reader in the same way a video topic trailer can. Trailers incorporate visual and auditory components, meaning that they appeal to more senses than a piece of writing would and take less time to watch than an informational essay usually does to read. Plus, some people engage differently in what they watch than what they read. Since video topic trailers are short and appeal to a variety of senses, they can get readers interested in a topic, which makes them then want to read the whole essay on that topic."

Next, I indicate that video topic trailers can enhance an audience's experience by introducing the viewers to key facts about the topic, explaining that they provide a "preview" that can both inform and engage readers. In these discussions, I like to emphasize how video topic trailers are engaging not only because of their use of multimedia, but also due to the information they contain. I explain that strong video topic trailers include especially important information about their topics that alert readers to important facts about the subject and pique their curiosity about it. "This is a great benefit to your audience," I recently told a group of students, "because it gives them an introduction to some especially important details, while also allowing them to think about what other information they'll learn. Since a video topic trailer highlights some important facts but doesn't go into a lot of detail, it lets readers know some big ideas you'll address and also gets them interested enough to read more."

By discussing both of these benefits of video topic trailers—engaging viewers in the piece's topic and introducing audiences to important facts about that topic—teachers can emphasize to their students the importance of using multimedia purposefully in their writing, helping them understand that integrating technology into one's work can have great value if the author clearly understands the positive impact of that technological innovation.

3. Give students suggestions for creating their own video topic trailers.

Now that the students have seen examples of video topic trailers and learned about ways they can enhance an audience's experience, they should be ready to consider suggestions for creating their own topic trailers. When I give students suggestions for creating video topic trailers, I focus on three tips: (1) select some especially significant facts about your topic to share in your video topic trailer, (2) use a storyboard to plan the visual images you'll display in your video, and (3) come up with a strong opening statement that you'll deliver in your video.

As illustrated in this chapter's classroom snapshot, I like to present each of these suggestions to students separately; after sharing each suggestion, I ask students to comment on why they think it could be important for creating an effective video topic trailer. This helps foster a student-centered discussion about each recommendation, which I've found to be much more effective than me simply telling the students what to do. For example, in the classroom snapshot section, I recount telling my students that it's important to craft a strong opening statement to deliver in a video topic trailer; after explaining what this recommendation means and giving an example of it, I ask students to share their thoughts on why it might be important in an effective video topic trailer. After the students share their comments, I recommend sharing any additional insights about the topic that they did not address; this ensures that the class discussion incorporates all the reasons why each recommendation is important. Figure 3.1 lists each of the suggestions discussed in this section and a key reason each one is significant.

Figure 3.1 Suggestions for Creating Video Topic Trailers

Suggestion	Why It's Important
Select some especially significant facts about your topic to share in your video topic trailer.	Selecting two or three especially important facts to share communicates key information to the audience without overwhelming them.
Use a storyboard to plan the visual images you'll display in your video.	Using a storyboard ensures that you'll have a plan for your video topic trailer before you start recording it and helps you visualize how the scenes in your trailer will look.
Create an opening statement to deliver in your video topic trailer.	A strong opening statement clearly communicates what your video is about and gets the viewer's attention.

4.   Work with students as they plan their own video topic trailers.

Next, I recommend checking in with students as they work independently to plan the video topic trailers they'll create. This planning process involves students composing scripts that contain everything they'll say in their videos and storyboards that depict the scenes that will appear in them. When conferring with my students, I use the three recommendations discussed in the previous section to guide the conversation. During a recent meeting with a student creating a video topic trailer on the James River (a river that runs through the Virginia town where she lives), I asked her questions drawn directly from the three previously described suggestions. I first asked her what especially significant facts she would share with the audience about the James River and why she felt those facts were particularly important. Next, I inquired into which visual images she'd display in her video and why she chose those scenes. Finally, I asked her what opening statement she will deliver in her topic trailer and how that opening statement communicates the video's topic while also getting the reader's attention. The chart depicted in Figure 3.2 provides a resource you can use when conferring with your students as they plan their video topic trailers; the left side of this chart features key questions to ask your students during these conferences, while the right side of the chart includes spaces to record your notes about their answers. (A reproducible version of this chart is also available in Appendix A.)

Figure 3.2 Conference Questions for Students Creating Video Topic Trailers

Questions to Ask Students during Conferences	Your Notes about Their Responses
What are some especially significant facts about your topic that you decided to share in your video topic trailer? Follow-up question: Why do you feel those facts are especially important?	
Which visual images will you display in your video topic trailer? Follow-up question: Why did you choose these scenes?	
What opening statement will you deliver in your video topic trailer? Follow-up question: How does that opening statement communicate the video's topic while also getting the reader's attention?	

5. Ask students to reflect on the beneficial components of the video topic trailers they created.

I recommend concluding this instructional process by asking your students to respond to a reflection question that calls for them to consider specific beneficial aspects of their video topic trailers: "What specific parts of your video topic trailer do you think your audience will most benefit from? Why?" I like how this question asks students to think about particular aspects of their own video topic trailers, requiring them to consider the precise choices they made in planning and recording their trailers. Throughout this instructional process, students consider the general benefits and features of video topic trailers, but this is the first time they are asked to reflect on the successful aspects of their own trailers and why those components were successful.

The student who created the previously discussed video topic trailer on hybrid cars indicated the following when reflecting on the aspects of his topic trailer that most benefit his audience: "Seeing so many parts of hybrid cars and hearing me talk about why they're important [can benefit the audience]. This shows them what all of these things look like and helps them see, not just read about, what makes hybrid cars so special." He then continued on why displaying these features can enhance the audience's understanding of the components of hybrid cars: "I think this can be helpful to the audience because it's hard to describe some of these [hybrid car parts] in words. This lets them see what the parts look like before they even start reading the essay. This can help them understand what I'm talking about."

Final Thoughts on Creating Video Topic Trailers

- A video topic trailer is a short film that a student creates about an informational writing topic.
- The topic trailer provides a kind of preview that conveys selected, high-interest details about the essay's subject and piques readers' curiosity levels about the topic.
- Creating video topic trailers for informational essays has a number of potential benefits; this activity requires students to
  - Identify key information in their works.
  - Reflect on how to use videos to engage potential readers.
  - Interact with their topics in unique ways.
- When teaching students about creating video topic trailers on informational writing topics,
  - Show students examples of video topic trailers that introduce informational writing topics.

- Talk with students about how video topic trailers can enhance an audience's experience.
- Give students suggestions for creating their own video topic trailers.
- Work with students as they plan their own video topic trailers.
- Ask students to reflect on the beneficial components of the video topic trailers they created.

4

Using Images and Figures to Aid Comprehension and Illustrate Concepts

In this chapter, we'll explore how students can enhance their informational writing by using images and figures to aid the reader's comprehension and further illustrate important concepts. First, we'll consider what this form of multimedia use entails and then examine how it can benefit informational writing. After that, we'll check out a description of a lesson I did with a fifth-grade class on this writing strategy, finally concluding by considering some key recommendations to keep in mind when helping your students incorporate images and figures in their informational works.

What Is It?

Authors of informational texts frequently rely on more than just written language to communicate ideas to their audiences; they also incorporate images and figures to help convey important information to their readers. Many informational authors include photos, illustrations, charts, graphs, and infographics to enhance readers' understanding of the piece's topic. You may be asking yourself, "Which of these images and figures are best to include in informational writing? Should authors include a bunch of them or just pick one?" The answer to this question depends on the individual author's objectives: one feature might best align with a particular context, while another feature might fit better with another kind of piece. For example, some of the students with whom I recently discussed this concept used a wide range of images and figures in their works: one student used a photo of an injured manatee to depict how motorboats can endanger manatees' lives, another used a graph to illustrate the changes in the number of giant pandas living in the wild, and yet another incorporated an infographic identifying important events from the career of hockey player Mario Lemieux. These examples represent the idea of using multimedia purposefully, as each image or figure aligns with its topic and gives readers a useful way to further understand that topic.

Why Is It Beneficial?

Images and figures such as photos, illustrations, charts, graphs, and infographics can benefit a piece of informational writing in two important and related ways: by highlighting important information for readers and helping readers understand that information. In each of the examples mentioned in the previous section—a photo of an injured manatee, a graph that shows changes in the giant panda population, and an infographic outlining the key events from a hockey star's career—the author used multimedia images and figures to emphasize key points about their topics and aid their readers' understanding of those points.

When talking with my students about the benefits of using images and figures in informational writing to illustrate concepts and aid comprehensions, I display a humorous infographic I created that compares my basketball skills and experiences with those of NBA superstar LeBron James and talk about its features. This infographic, depicted in Figure 4.1, makes a number of humorous, self-deprecating points about my lack of basketball background and ability (highlighting information such as me never having played on any basketball team, the fact that many fifth graders possess better basketball skills than I do, and my below-average height) and compares them to LeBron James's accomplishments and attributes.

I discuss the infographic with my students, pointing out that it would enhance an essay on this topic by highlighting key facts and helping readers understand those facts. "If I wrote an essay comparing my experiences in basketball with LeBron James's," I explained in a recent conversation with a group of fifth graders, "I would use this infographic to enhance readers' comprehension of the essay; it highlights the differences between LeBron James and me, calling attention to our basketball experiences, skills levels, and height. In addition, the infographic makes it easier for readers to understand these differences because of the clear and organized way it presents and compares the information."

To further illustrate the importance of incorporating images and figures in informational writing, I show my students the table depicted in Figure 4.2, which identifies and explains the two major benefits of using multimedia in this way.

Figure 4.1 Sean Ruday versus LeBron James Comparison Infographic

I've found that this table provides students with a clear and organized explanation of how images and figures can enhance their informational works, emphasizing the idea that writers do not incorporate this form of multimedia (or any other) simply for the sake of doing so, but rather because it has the potential to enhance the effectiveness of their works. Next, we'll take a look inside a fifth-grade classroom and examine a discussion I had with my students about this form of multimedia integration.

A Classroom Snapshot

I begin the day's discussion by telling my fifth graders, "I'm so proud of the wonderful work you all have done this week. Today, we're going to keep going with our discussion of using images and figures in your informational writing. I can't wait to hear what you have to say!"

Today marks the third class in which these fifth graders and I have discussed the writing strategy of incorporating images and figures into their informational writing. First, I introduced the students to this concept, explaining what it means to include images and figures in informational writing and showing them some examples of what this can look like in practice. In our second meeting, the students and I talked about the benefits of purposefully used images and figures, discussing how the examples I showed them can enhance a piece of informational writing and examining the explanations of the benefits explored in Figure 4.2. In today's class, I'm going to prepare the students to incorporate this strategy into their own works by providing them with three tips to keep in mind when using images and figures in their informational writings.

After providing the students with an overview of the day's agenda, I then jump into the recommendations: "The first tip I have for you as you think about including images and figures in your informational writing is to make sure to use the kinds of images and/or figures that best fit with the points you make in your essay. This means thinking about the message you want to get across to your readers and asking yourself what type of images get that message across best. For example, let's think about the infographic I recently showed you all that compares my basketball experiences and abilities with LeBron James. Since this figure compares two things, I'd use it in an essay that focuses on making these comparisons so that the figure would fit with the topic I'm describing. Does that make sense so far?"

Figure 4.2 Benefits of Incorporating Images and Figures into Informational Writing

Benefit	Explanation
Highlighting important information for readers	Images and figures can identify and emphasize key facts, ideas, and concepts, ensuring that this information stands out to the essay's readers.
Helping readers understand important information	The details contained in informational images and figures (such as the image depicted in a photograph, the concepts presented in a chart, or the events outlined on a timeline) help ensure that readers comprehend the identified information.

"Yeah," responds a student. "The essay compares LeBron and you, so you'd use a figure that also compares LeBron and you."

"Exactly," I reply. "The figure would align with the message of the essay. Let's think of another example: If I was writing an essay about the history of basketball, I would use different kinds of images and figures—ones that would best fit with the points of that essay. If I wanted to help readers understand what basketball hoops looked like when the sport first started, I'd include a photo of basketball hoops from this time. How do you all think this photo would best fit with the point of that essay?"

A number of students raise their hands; I call on a young lady who shares, "The photo would go with the point [of the essay] because [the essay] is describing the history of basketball and the photo would show part of the history of basketball."

"Very nice analysis," I tell the student. "That photo would definitely go along with the point of the essay. Now, I'm going to share the second tip I have for you as you think about using images and figures in your essays: make sure the images and/or figures you use highlight important information in the essay. This is pretty logical when you think about it: if you're going to use an image or figure in your essay, it wouldn't make much sense for that image or figure to depict something that's not a very important part of the essay. Let's think about the example of the essay about the history of basketball. If I'm talking about changes in the equipment people used and the way they played, it wouldn't make such sense for me to include images or figures about something unrelated to that, like changes in players' hairstyles. Why do you all think it's important to make sure the images and figures you use highlight significant information in an essay?"

I smile, pleased at the number of student hands in the air; I call on a student who asserts, "I think it's because the images and figures would be confusing if they didn't highlight significant information, like in the example you talked about, where the essay would be about changes in equipment and how people played and the image was about hairstyles. This wouldn't really make sense and would probably be confusing. If the images and figures highlight significant information in the essay, they make a lot more sense to the reader."

"That's a really nice point," I explain. "If the images and figures in an essay don't relate to the essay's main points, they'll confuse readers rather than help them. We want the images and figures we use to help readers make sense of our written works; this can only happen if those features align with the essay's main ideas."

"I have one more suggestion to share with you all," I continue. "This one builds off the last one we just discussed and takes the ideas in that suggestion to an even higher level of usefulness. When including images and figures in your informational writing, make sure that the multimedia you incorporate helps readers understand important information in your essay. Let's connect this idea to the last one: In our last suggestion, we talked about making sure your images and figures relate to important information in your essay. While that's really important, I also want you to keep in mind that images and figures are most useful if they help readers understand this information."

"Let's think back to the example where I compared myself to LeBron James," I tell the students. "In that graphic, I highlighted important information that I'd discuss in an essay about LeBron and me. However, I also did something more than that: I helped readers understand this information by presenting it in an easy-to-understand graphic that clearly compared these points. If I used a graphic that addressed important details but didn't present them in a way that was easy for readers to understand, that graphic wouldn't be very useful to my readers. What are some ways you all think we can make images and figures that help readers understand important information?"

"You can use graphics that compare facts, like you did in that example," answers one student. "The graphics can help readers understand the things you're comparing."

"Absolutely right," I praise the student. "Figures like the infographic we examined can certainly help readers understand and compare important facts. What are some other ways that images and figures can help readers understand information?"

"A photograph can help," responds another student, "because it can show what something looks like."

"Great insight," I reply. "A photograph can, like you said, show readers what something looks like. We can connect this to our earlier conversation about using a photo of a basketball hoop from the days when the game first started to help readers understand what the equipment was like at that time."

I continue, "Another way to help readers understand information is through a graph that reveals change over time. I know some people in our class are writing about endangered species; a graph that shows change over time could help with an essay on a topic like that by showing how the population of an endangered animal species has diminished over time."

A number of students nod; one interjects, "I'm going to do that!"

"Awesome!" I exclaim. "You all have done a great job today of considering and analyzing these suggestions I've shared with you. In our next class, I'll ask you to begin considering how you'll use images and figures to enhance your informational essays. See you tomorrow!"

Recommendations for Teaching Students about Using Images and Figures to Aid Comprehension and Illustrate Concepts

In this section, I describe a step-by-step instructional process to use when teaching students about using images and figures in their informational essays to aid readers' comprehension and illustrate concepts. The instructional steps I recommend are (1) show students examples of images and figures used in informational writing, (2) help students understand how images and figures can benefit informational writing, (3) provide students with recommendations for incorporating images and figures into their own works, (4) confer with students as they integrate images and figures into their informational writing, and (5) have students reflect on the impact of the images and figures they used in their own pieces. Each of these recommendations is described in detail in this section.

1. Show students examples of images and figures used in informational writing.

This opening step forms the foundation for the rest of this instructional process, providing students with concrete examples of what images and figures used in informational writing can look like. Once students have seen models of these multimedia forms, they'll be able to think in more complex and abstract terms about how images and figures can enhance a piece of writing and how writers can use them as purposefully as possible. I like to show students a figure I've made (such as the previously described infographic example comparing LeBron James and me) so that they can see how authors might create their own examples that align with the information in their own essays. It's important to note that these teacher-created figures don't need to be complicated infographics to provide students with effective examples: straightforward charts or tables can illustrate how informational authors use figures to aid readers' understanding of important ideas. It's also a good idea to show students some images (such as photos or illustrations) that clearly depict concepts that authors of informational texts may want their readers to understand; providing examples of images emphasizes that these multimedia forms can also be effective ways to aid comprehension and enhance readers' experiences.

In addition to showing students teacher-created images and figures, it's also a great idea to point to some published sources so that students can see how this multimedia tool is used in real-world writing. The website "Time for Kids" (which is affiliated with *Time* magazine) has high-interest informational articles that incorporate many forms of multimedia, such as images, figures, and tables. For example, this site published an article in June 2016 about the world's longest and deepest rail tunnel, which had recently opened in Switzerland. The article included photos, including one of a train emerging from the tunnel, and a graph conveying information about some of the other longest tunnels in the world. Appendix C contains a link to the "Time for Kids" website as well as a link to this specific article.

2. Help students understand how images and figures can benefit informational writing.

This second step builds off of the information presented in the first: now that you've shown students examples of images and figures that can be included in informational writing, you can talk with them about how those images and figures can enhance the written works in which they appear. I like to begin my discussion of the benefits of this multimedia use by returning to the examples I showed them in the previous recommendation: "You've already seen what images and figures in informational writing can look like," I tell the students, "but now we're going to think about how they can make a piece of informational writing better."

When discussing with your students the benefits of incorporating images and figures, I recommend emphasizing the two key benefits addressed in Figure 4.2: (1) highlighting important information for readers and (2) helping readers understand important information. I suggest explaining how these two benefits are distinct ideas but also have some important commonalities: an effective figure first identifies and emphasizes important information and then uses its features to help readers understand that information. A teacher I recently observed helped her students comprehend these benefits. While displaying a flowchart that identified the sequence of events in the water cycle and the order in which they occurred, she noted that this graphic not only identified important details from the essay on the water cycle in which it appeared but also increased the likelihood that readers would understand these details. "When this is done well," she said, referring to the use of images and figures in informational writing, "it points out important things in your essay *and* helps readers understand those things." This statement perfectly summarizes the key benefits of this multimedia use.

3. Provide students with recommendations for incorporating images and figures into their own works.

One of my favorite parts of this instructional process is when the students have grasped what it means to incorporate images and figures in their informational writing and are aware of the benefits of this strategy, as this means they've developed a strong understanding of this multimedia use and are close to being able to integrate it into their own writings. Before they do so, though, it's important to provide students with recommendations for incorporating images and figures into their own works. As discussed in this chapter's classroom snapshot, the three recommendations I give students are (1) make sure to use the kinds of images and/or figures that best fit with the points you make in your essay, (2) make sure the images and/or figures you use highlight important information in the essay, and (3) make sure that the multimedia you incorporate helps readers understand important information in your essay.

These suggestions, which extend logically from the benefits of incorporating images and figures in informational writing, provide students with important strategies for making the images and figures they include in their works as beneficial as possible. When I present each suggestion, I make connections to the examples of images and figures I've already shown my students to provide a concrete reference point for the idea I'm sharing. In addition, I like to ask my students for their thoughts on why each recommendation is an important idea for writers to keep in mind; this helps me gauge their understanding and lets me know the extent to which I should further explain the significance of the suggestions.

4. Confer with students as they integrate images and figures into their informational writing.

At this point in the instructional process, the students are ready to take on more ownership by working independently to integrate images and figures into their works. While they do so, I recommend conferring with them individually to monitor their progress and provide any needed individualized support. For example, if a figure doesn't align with the main points of a student's essay or is hard to understand, I'll make suggestions to help the student maximize the effectiveness of the figure.

I recently conferred with a student who was writing an informational piece on the career of retired hockey player Mario Lemieux; this student chose to integrate a timeline of the major events of Lemieux's career to highlight important information in his essay and help readers understand that information. The timeline this student created is depicted in Figure 4.3.

In this conference, I didn't need to provide any revision suggestions, as this student's figure does a great job of providing information that aligns with his essay's main point, highlighting key facts and helping readers understand those facts.

5. Have students reflect on the impact of the images and figures they used in their own pieces.

I like to conclude this instructional process by asking students to reflect on how the images and figures they incorporated into their works impacted their pieces. This reflection activity enhances students' abilities to think metacognitively about the importance of this form of technology integration by helping them consider the difference it makes in the effectiveness of their informational writing. To achieve this goal, I ask my students two related reflection questions: (1) How do you think the images and/or figures you incorporated into your informational writing enhanced the piece? (2) What might a reader's experience be like without these components? Asking students these reflection questions about the significance of images and figures to their informational works emphasizes the idea that technological tools should be used purposefully and with an understanding of their benefits.

Figure 4.3 Timeline of Important Events in Mario Lemieux's Career

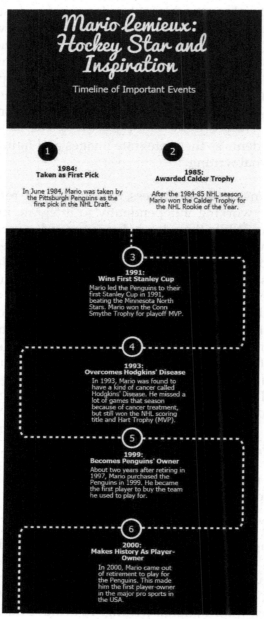

The student who created the timeline depicted in Figure 4.3 asserted that this infographic made a significant impact on his essay: "My timeline about important events in Mario's life made my essay better because the timeline helped the readers understand that these events were really important and why they were so important. Without them, sure the essay would still describe the events, but there wouldn't be this timeline really focusing on how important they are." I love that this student's comment shows his awareness of the fact that his essay describes the events featured in his timeline but the timeline still enhances the piece by calling attention to the important events in a hockey player's life and conveying their importance to the reader. These reflection statements illustrate the student's awareness of how this multimedia use enhances the effectiveness of his informational piece.

Final Thoughts on Using Images and Figures to Aid Comprehension and Illustrate Concepts

- ◆ Authors of informational text frequently incorporate images and figures to help convey important information to their readers.
- ◆ Examples of these images and figures include photos, illustrations, charts, graphs, and infographics to enhance readers' understanding of the piece's topic.
- ◆ Images and figures can benefit a piece of informational writing in two important and related ways:
  - ◆ By highlighting important information for readers
  - ◆ By helping readers understand important information
- ◆ When teaching students about using images and figures to aid comprehension and illustrate concepts,
  - ◆ Show students examples of images and figures used in informational writing.
  - ◆ Help students understand how images and figures can benefit informational writing.
  - ◆ Provide students with recommendations for incorporating images and figures into their own works.
  - ◆ Confer with students as they integrate images and figures into their informational writing.
  - ◆ Have students reflect on the impact of the images and figures they used in their own pieces.

Section **3**

Incorporating Multimedia into
Narrative Writing

5

Using Images, Videos, and Audio Files as Tools for Characterization

In this chapter, we'll explore an innovative and exciting way for students to incorporate multimedia into narrative writing: the use of images, videos, and audio files as tools for characterization. First, we'll consider what this strategy is and then think together about why it can enhance the pieces students create. Once we've done these things, we'll look inside a classroom where I helped students understand how to apply this strategy to their works. Finally, we'll examine five key recommendations to keep in mind when helping your students use images, videos, and audio files as tools for characterization in their narratives.

What Is It?

The use of images, videos, and audio files to enhance characterization in narrative writing is an outstanding example of the possibilities and potential associated with incorporating multimedia into student writing and writing instruction; it enables student writers to use these forms of multimedia to complement their written descriptions of characters. It's important to note that these images, videos, and audio files are not intended to take the place of traditional characterization strategies, such as written descriptions of characters' actions, thoughts, and dialogue that convey important information about them. Instead, this application of multimedia is meant to build off of written characterization, using these technological features to further develop the ideas in the written descriptions of characters.

When I introduce this strategy to students, I talk with them about the specific ways it can appear in a piece of narrative writing, explaining that an author can use an image or a link to a video or audio file to help reveal something important about a character's personality, motivation, or interest. For example, I recently worked with a student writing a narrative about a girl who dreamed of performing on Broadway. In the student's piece, the protagonist created this goal after hearing the song "Defying Gravity" in the musical *Wicked*; she included a link to a YouTube video of a performer in *Wicked* singing this song to emphasize its significance to the protagonist and ensure readers' understanding of it. Another student with whom I worked wrote a piece about a football player who listened to the song "Hall of Fame" by the musical group The Script before every game. He included a link to an audio file of that song so that readers could know what this song was like and understand the character better.

Why Is It Beneficial?

Now that we've considered ways of using multimedia to develop characterization, let's think about why it can benefit a piece of narrative writing. The purposeful use of images, videos, and audio files as tools of characterization can emphasize important ideas, ensure readers' understanding, and make a text as engaging as possible. Let's look at each of these benefits individually.

Emphasize Important Ideas

When I explain the benefits of this multimedia use to my students, I begin with the point that incorporating images, videos, and audio files can help authors emphasize important ideas in their works. In each of the student work examples discussed in the preceding section, the songs included in the students' narratives represented important aspects of the pieces in which they appeared: "Defying Gravity" was the source of one character's motivation to perform on Broadway, while the song "Hall of Fame" was part of another character's pregame football routine. It's important to note that students who include images, videos, and audio files in their writing should only do so when discussing entities that are especially important to their works. Including a multimedia clip of a song, for example, gives extra emphasis to that song, so an author should only do this when the song is especially important to the story (as in the previously described examples). If the song doesn't play a major role in the narrative, the author is better off not incorporating a multimedia version of it in the piece.

Ensure Readers' Understanding

The next benefit of this multimedia use I point out to my students is that using images, videos, and audio files as tools for characterization can also ensure that readers understand information that is important to the characters and the story. The student who used an audio file of the song "Hall of Fame" in his story shared his agreement with this idea: "This song's really important to Jay [the story's main character]. If I didn't include it, people who didn't know the song would just be like, 'What is that song?' Since it's in the story, people can just click on the link and hear it themselves." I explain to my students that including these forms of multimedia can make a piece of writing as accessible as possible: "Some of your readers might know about a certain song or image you're talking about in your story, while others might not. Using multimedia to show readers what the thing you're talking about sounds or looks like gives everyone the opportunity to understand it."

Make a Text as Engaging as Possible

The third and final benefit I discuss with my students is that incorporating multimedia in this way can make a text as engaging as possible for readers. As I explain in this book's introduction, today's students often read articles online that contain both written text and various forms of multimedia such as images and videos; incorporating these forms of multimedia allows students to create pieces that reflect the high-interest texts they encounter in their out-of-school lives and maximize their appeal for other readers. I tell my students that images, videos, and audio files that enhance reader engagement aren't meant to take the place of the written word; they're instead meant to provide readers with an additional way to interact with the content: "Including a YouTube clip, a picture, or a link to an audio files doesn't mean you don't need to write about that thing. It's doesn't replace your writing," I emphasize. "What it does is it allows your readers to get involved with your topic as much as possible." The two student examples discussed so far in this chapter are good examples of this benefit—the links the students included to the songs in their works can increase readers' engagement with their narratives without taking away from the written language in the song.

Now that we've explored each of the benefits of using multimedia as a characterization tool, let's look inside a fourth-grade classroom and check out a snapshot of my experiences working with students on this topic.

A Classroom Snapshot

"I think this is the coolest thing we've ever done in language arts," a student tells me at the beginning of class. "These things we've been talking about are really fun."

"I'm so happy to hear that!" I exclaim. "Today, we're going to continue the work we've been doing the past couple of classes."

For the past two days, these students and I have been exploring the idea of incorporating multimedia such as images, videos, and audio files into narrative writing as a tool for characterization. In our first meeting, I explained this strategy to the students, talking with them about how authors can use these multimedia forms to enhance characterization and providing examples of how this can look in practice. Next, in our second class on this topic, I spoke with the students about how this strategy can benefit a piece of narrative, identifying how it can emphasize important ideas, ensure readers' understanding, and make a text as engaging as possible.

"Today," I explain to my students, "is when we take this idea to an even higher level because we're going to start talking about some ways to include images, videos, and audio in your own narratives to help with characterization. I'm going to share with you three recommendations to keep in mind when using these types of multimedia to enhance the characterization in your own writing. Then, in our next class, we're going to start including these multimedia forms in our narrative writing. Does that sound good?"

"Yeah," responds one student. "I'm excited for this."

"Awesome!" I exclaim. "After today, you'll definitely be ready to apply it to your writing." I then share the following three suggestions with the students:

◆ Make sure that the multimedia you include shows important information about the character.
◆ Make sure that this multimedia can help readers better understand what you describe in the text.
◆ Make sure that the multimedia doesn't replace the written description in your narrative.

"Let's talk about these together, starting with the first one," I continue. "For each of these, we're going to think about what it means and why it's important. We're going to start with the first suggestion: Make sure that the multimedia you include shows important information about the character. This means that, if you're using multimedia to help with characterization in your narrative, you want to be sure this multimedia shows readers something meaningful about the character you're describing, like his or her personality, goals, or interests. Remember the example I showed you that I wrote about a young basketball player?"

A number of students nod, recalling a model of this strategy featuring highlights of basketball star LeBron James that I showed them in our first conversation on the topic. "Do you remember what multimedia I used as a characterization tool in that story?"

"I do!" interjects a student. "You talked about how the main character watched highlights of LeBron James every night before going to bed and put links to those highlights in the story."

"Exactly," I reply. "Does anyone remember what those LeBron James highlights showed us about the story's protagonist?"

"They showed how much he cares about basketball and how much he wants to be as great as LeBron," answers a student.

"That's absolutely right," I praise the student's comment. "I included those examples of multimedia with a specific goal in mind: I wanted to make sure the multimedia I used there showed, like you just mentioned, how much Luke, the story's protagonist, is dedicated to being a successful basketball player. As this example we just talked about can show, the recommendation I shared with you—make sure that the multimedia you include shows important information about the character—is a really important thing to think about. If you use multimedia to help with characterization, make sure that the multimedia you're using helps readers understand the character better and that it gives important information about what the character enjoys, is interested in, or is like as a person."

"Now," I explain, "we're going to think about the second recommendation I have for you today, which is to make sure that the multimedia you use can help readers better understand what you describe in the text. In other words, sometimes you might describe something in your narrative that all of your readers might not totally understand, like a song or a video clip. Some readers who are familiar with the topic might understand, but some of them, like perhaps old people like me"—this elicits a giggle from several students—"might not. For example, let's think about the narrative that we just discussed in which the protagonist shows his interest in basketball in part by watching LeBron James highlights. Since some readers might not be very familiar with LeBron James and his level of basketball skill, the video clip of these highlights can help all readers understand what's being described, even if they're not really familiar with it."

"I think I get it," states a student. "Like if I want to put a Justin Bieber song in my story to go along with how much my character loves Justin Bieber and his music, that song will help everyone know the song I'm talking about, even if they didn't know of it before."

"Absolutely right," I respond. "If you're talking about something in your narrative that's really important to the story and you think all readers might not understand it, you can incorporate a multimedia link to or image of it if possible. This can help all of your readers understand what you're describing, which can really help everyone reading your narrative enjoy it as much as possible. I'll talk with you about this idea even more in our one-on-one conferences when you start working on doing this on your own."

"The last recommendation I have for you today is a little bit of a different one," I inform the students. "The first two suggestions we've discussed are things *to* do; this one is something *not* to do: if you use multimedia to enhance the characterization in your narrative, make sure that the multimedia used doesn't replace the written description in your narrative. You want to make sure you describe important ideas in your narrative in writing and then use the multimedia to provide extra detail and clarification;

this allows the multimedia to play a supporting role, not a lead role, in your narrative. For example, let's think about my narrative about Luke, the basketball player: I wrote about Luke watching highlights of LeBron James to motivate himself and learn more about basketball. After writing about this, I included links to those highlights so readers can access them. What I *didn't* do, though, is just put the highlight links in the narrative without explaining them first. Now, let's hear some of your thoughts. Why do you all think it's important that the multimedia in a narrative supports the writing but doesn't overtake it?"

A number of hands shoot up around the room; I call on a student who shares, "It's important because you don't want the story to just be a bunch of links. It should be your writing, and then the links can add extra information."

"Yeah," adds another student. "It's the author's story, so the author should be doing the writing. If the author's putting in a lot of links but not writing much, the author isn't really telling the story."

A third student contributes to the conversation, explaining, "I think it's important because the description of the character starts with what the author writes and then the multimedia can give extra detail."

"Very well said, all of you," I proclaim. "I really like how thoughtfully and insightfully you commented on the importance of the author owning the work and the writing being the most important thing, with the multimedia providing extra information. Great work today—tomorrow we'll get started on you all putting these ideas into action in your own writings!"

Recommendations for Teaching Students about Using Images, Videos, and Audio Files as Tools for Characterization

In this section, I describe a step-by-step instructional process to use when teaching students about using images, videos, and audio files to enhance characterization in their narrative writing. The instructional steps I recommend are (1) show students examples of narratives that use multimedia as tools for characterization; (2) talk with students about how purposefully used images, videos, and audio files can benefit a piece of narrative writing; (3) provide students with suggestions for incorporating multimedia into their own narratives; (4) work with students as they use multimedia to enhance characterization in their pieces; and (5) have students reflect on the effectiveness of using images, videos, and audio files as tools for characterization in their narratives. Each of these recommendations is described in detail in this section.

1. Show students examples of narratives that use multimedia as tools for characterization.

Figure 5.1 Excerpt from "Be Like LeBron"

"It's time for bed, Luke," Mom reminded me. She knows what's up, though—in my world, "time for bed" isn't just the quick actions of brushing teeth, putting on pajamas, and that sort of thing.

No, for me, getting ready for bed involves what I call my "goals time." After doing what "normal" people do at bedtime, I high-five my LeBron James Fathead and fire up my LeBron highlight videos—I've found a whole YouTube Channel of LeBron highlights; I watch 10 minutes of them every night before turning off my computer and lights and then drifting off to sleep. That night, I watched my favorite video, the one that shows him coasting from one end of the court to the other and dunking on these two helpless defenders.

I strongly recommend beginning the instructional process by showing students what this multimedia use looks like in action; I've found that once students can grasp what it means to use multimedia to facilitate characterization, the rest of the process flows well. To maximize students' understanding of this multimedia use, I suggest showing them at least one example of what it can look like in practice. When working with the class described in this chapter, I began our first conversation on the topic by showing them the previously discussed narrative about a young basketball player named Luke who watched video highlights of LeBron James every night before bed.

Figure 5.1 depicts an excerpt from that narrative; it describes Luke's evening routine, which is meant to convey his interest in and dedication to basketball.

After I show students this excerpt, I share with them the video to which Luke refers and explain that, in a completed version of the narrative, I would include a link to it so that readers can fully understand the situation and grasp Luke's interests and goals as clearly as possible. When working with your students, you can show them this excerpt to help them grasp how this multimedia use can look in practice. It's also a great idea to create your own example—students love seeing their teachers' writing; it can bolster the sense of community in your classroom and help them feel like they, too, can complete a challenging task.

2. Talk with students about how purposefully used images, videos, and audio files can benefit a piece of narrative writing.

Once you've shown students an example of this strategy in practice, I recommend moving your discussion to a higher level by helping students understand how using multimedia as a characterization tool can enhance a piece of narrative writing. When I talk with my students about this idea, I focus on the benefits described earlier in this chapter: emphasizing important ideas, ensuring readers' understanding, and making a text as engaging as possible. I like to do so by returning to the example I showed the students in the previous recommendation and identifying specific ways it achieves each of these benefits; this gives students a concrete connection to each of these benefits.

For example, I'll explain to students that the video of LeBron James referred to in the preceding section achieves the first benefit by emphasizing an important idea and calling attention to Luke's passion for basketball and admiration of LeBron James. "Luke's interest in and dedication to basketball are important parts of this story," I tell the students, "and this use of multimedia emphasizes that." Next, I'll focus on the second benefit, explaining how this video ensures readers' understanding of key information. In my story about Luke, the video I include provides readers with a clear understanding of what the highlights he watches look like and the kind of basketball player Luke aspires to be. "It's possible that not all of the readers will be able to picture what highlights of LeBron James playing basketball might look like," I recently explained to my students. "Putting this video link in the story allows everyone to understand what Luke watches." Finally, I talk with my students about how this multimedia can benefit the piece by making it as engaging as possible: "Including a link to some LeBron highlights allows readers to interact with the narrative in a different way. It gives the story another dimension." When I discuss this benefit, I make a point of emphasizing that the multimedia can add another element to the piece but isn't meant to replace the written text.

3. Provide students with suggestions for incorporating multimedia into their own narratives.

The next step of this instructional process involves preparing students to incorporate multimedia into their own works by providing them with specific recommendations to follow while doing so. The recommendations I give my students are discussed in this chapter's snapshot: (1) make sure that the multimedia you include shows important information about the character, (2) make sure that this multimedia can help readers better understand what you describe in the text, and (3) make sure that the multimedia doesn't replace the written description in your narrative.

As illustrated in the snapshot, I explain each suggestion to my students, making as many specific connections as possible to the example of multimedia integration I've shown them. I also like to ask students to comment on why they think each recommendation is an important one to follow. This facilitates the students' in-depth thinking about the ideas presented to them, thereby increasing the likelihood that they'll follow those recommendations. For example, after presenting my students with the idea that multimedia should complement but not replace written description, I asked them to comment on it: "Now, let's hear some of your thoughts. Why do you all think it's important that the multimedia in a narrative supports it but doesn't overtake it?" Students' responses to questions like this one can help you evaluate their level of understanding, while also requiring them to think carefully and analytically about the ideas you share with them.

4. Work with students as they use multimedia to enhance characterization in their pieces.

The fourth part of this instructional process is one of the most exciting: it's when you get to hold one-on-one conferences with students as they work to use multimedia to enhance the characterization in their narratives. When I hold these conferences, I use the suggestions I provided in the previous step to guide the conversations by asking students questions about how their multimedia integration aligns with each of these suggestions. The chart depicted in Figure 5.2 contains the questions I ask my students in these conversations as well as places where I record my notes about their answers. (A reproducible version of this chart is also available in Appendix A.)

As students respond to my questions, I like to make notes about what they do particularly well, what follow-up questions I should ask, and what suggestions I'll give them to use this multimedia as effectively as possible. This allows me to make my instruction personalized to their needs, which is especially important in such an individualized task.

When conferring with the previously mentioned student who incorporated a link to a YouTube clip of the song "Defying Gravity" from the musical *Wicked*, I noted that she did a great job of using this video to show important information about the character but also commented that she could do an even better job of balancing the multimedia with written description: "I love

Figure 5.2 Conference Questions for Students Using Multimedia to Enhance Characterization

Questions to Ask Students during Conferences	Your Notes about Their Responses
How does the multimedia you include show important information about the character?	
How does the multimedia you include help readers better understand what you describe in the text?	
How does the multimedia you include add to your narrative without replacing written descriptions?	

your use of this 'Defying Gravity' video because it shows such an important part of the protagonist's identity, but I also want you to make sure you don't use it to replace the written description in the piece. Expand more in writing on why this song is important to Isabelle [the story's protagonist] and then include the link. This will help balance out the narrative." The one-on-one conference this student and I had helped me provide her with this individualized instruction, designed to maximize the quality of her work.

5. Have students reflect on the effectiveness of using images, videos, and audio files as tools for characterization in their narratives.

This final step may be the most important of all five in this process. This may seem somewhat counterintuitive, as it doesn't involve the students actually integrating multimedia into their works. However, this step does involve something that I and other proponents of metacognition believe to be just as important as actually using a writing strategy: students reflecting on the impact of that strategy on their own works. To guide students as they reflect on the importance of using multimedia as a tool for characterization, I ask them two related questions: (1) What positive impact do you think using multimedia as a tool for characterization had on your narrative? (2) How do you think your narrative would be different if you didn't use multimedia as a tool for characterization?

After completing her narrative, the student who incorporated a link to a performance of the song "Defying Gravity" thoughtfully reflected on these questions. Answering the first question, she explained, "It made a big difference! I think putting the link to 'Defying Gravity' in the story made the story more fun for readers and made sure that everyone understood what the song is. The song's really important to Isabelle, so everyone reading needs to understand the song to know about her." This explanation not only shows the student author's awareness of the impact of this multimedia use on her piece but also reveals her understanding of the benefits in general of using multimedia to facilitate characterization. In response to the second question, she noted, "If I didn't use this song, people who didn't already know the song would have been confused or just wouldn't have understood it as well. They probably wouldn't have had as much fun either, since they couldn't listen to such a great song!"

Final Thoughts on Using Images, Videos, and Audio Files as Tools for Characterization

◆ The use of images, videos, and audio files to enhance characterization in narrative writing enables student writers to use these forms of multimedia to complement their written descriptions of characters.

- When I introduce this strategy to students, I talk with them about the specific ways it can appear in a piece of narrative writing, explaining that an author can use an image or a link to a video or audio file to help reveal something important about a character's personality, motivation, or interest.
- The purposeful use of images, videos, and audio files as tools of characterization can benefit a piece of narrative writing by
  - Emphasizing important ideas
  - Ensuring readers' understanding
  - Making a text as engaging as possible
- When teaching students about using images, videos, and audio files as tools for characterization in their own writing,
  - Show students examples of narratives that use multimedia as tools for characterization.
  - Talk with students about how purposefully used images, videos, and audio files can benefit a piece of narrative writing.
  - Provide students with suggestions for incorporating multimedia into their own narratives.
  - Work with students as they use multimedia to enhance characterization in their pieces.
  - Have students reflect on the effectiveness of using images, videos, and audio files as tools for characterization in their narratives.

6

Incorporating Multimedia That Captures Thematic Elements

Another effective and innovative use of multimedia in narrative writing is using images, videos, and audio files to capture thematic elements. In this chapter, we'll examine what this strategy is and how it can benefit students' narrative writing. We'll then check out a description of a lesson I did with a group of third graders on this concept. Finally, we'll consider some recommendations to keep in mind when helping your students incorporate multimedia that captures thematic elements into their narratives.

What Is It?

In this form of multimedia integration, authors incorporate images, videos, and audio files that reflect a theme or central idea of their narrative in some way. This strategy differs from the idea discussed in the preceding chapter (using multimedia as a tool for characterization) because this concept uses multimedia to convey themes or main ideas in a piece (such as independence, friendship, or equality), while Chapter Five explained how to use multimedia to reveal a character's personality, motivation, or interest.

There are a variety of ways student writers can use multimedia to express themes or central ideas in their works. One student with whom I've worked incorporated a variety of forms, using both an image and an audio file to emphasize key elements of her narrative about a soccer player: "I used a photo of a soccer field at night that had just one player practicing on it. I picked it because the theme of my story is dedication and that picture really shows dedication, I think. I also used a clip of the song 'Roar' by Katy Perry because I think that song is totally about dedication also."

Figure 6.1 Student Narrative Excerpt

That afternoon, Kyle walked through the forest for another hour until he finally saw the houses of his neighborhood. He first noticed the house of one of his neighbors and then recognized his. "At first, I didn't want to go on this outdoor adventure," he thought to himself. "Now, I don't want it to end." He thanked his older brother for taking him on this journey and thought about how things would be different in his life. "I know I look the same and sound the same," he said, "but now I'm not afraid of the things that scared me before. This journey made me a different person."

Another student writer used a photograph of the woods to convey the idea "that the outdoors can really have a big impact on you." He explained, "My story's about a kid named Kyle who goes on an adventure in the outdoors. When his adventure's done, he thinks about things really differently, like he's a lot braver and more independent. At the end of my story, after the final paragraph, I put in a picture I took of these really awesome trees in the woods. I think these trees, since they're so awesome looking, help show the idea that the outdoors is a place that can have a big impact on you." Figure 6.1 depicts the final paragraph of this student's narrative and the photograph to which he refers.

Why Is It Beneficial?

Now that we've examined how this writing strategy can look in practice, let's consider how it can benefit students' narrative writing: the use of multimedia to reflect themes or central ideas of narratives can aid readers' comprehension and enhance their levels of engagement. In this section, we'll take a look at each of these benefits individually.

Multimedia Can Aid Readers' Comprehension of Narratives

The use of photos, videos, and audio files that convey themes and/or central ideas of narratives can have a powerful impact on readers' understanding of the works. While the text itself should illustrate these important ideas, related multimedia can provide readers with additional means of comprehending them. To illustrate this thought, let's consider the two examples described in the previous section. In the narrative about a soccer player training hard and displaying her determination, the two forms of multimedia integrated into this work emphasized this idea: both the image the student used of a lone soccer player training at night and the link to Katy Perry's song "Roar" emphasize the theme of determination that is central to the piece. The student who created this piece noted that, although readers can grasp this theme through the written text alone, the multimedia helped convey this idea: "Someone can just read my story and understand that the theme is dedication, but the [multimedia] can help people understand that dedication is the main idea of the story because the picture and the song are also about [dedication]." The author of the other piece of student work described in the preceding section, a narrative that emphasizes the power of nature, also commented on how the multimedia he used can help readers comprehend his piece's central idea: "In my story, I write about how the outdoors had a big impact on Kyle, but the photograph I put in there also shows the impact the outdoors can have on somebody. The trees in the picture, and how awesome they are, can help show the impact of the outdoors."

Multimedia Can Enhance Readers' Levels of Engagement

In addition to facilitating comprehension, the use of multimedia to convey thematic elements can appeal to readers by making the narratives in which the multimedia is used more interactive and engaging. Frey, Fisher, and Gonzalez (2010) explain that students can maximize the appeal and accessibility of their written works by incorporating technological innovations; the use of theme-based multimedia to engage readers is an excellent example of this, as it can enhance readers' interests in a piece of writing by giving them a chance to investigate related technology-based content. However, I tell my students that this benefit is only really achieved when the multimedia is used purposefully: "Using multimedia won't interest your readers very much if you use it all the time," I explain to them. "It's best to pick just one or two carefully selected examples of multimedia that perfectly capture a central idea or major theme in your narrative. It can be fun to click on a link to a song that's related to the story or to look at an image that captures the story's main idea. Remember, though, that having a whole bunch of multimedia is just distracting and possibly annoying; your reader might be overwhelmed and forget that you've written anything at all. However, if you have just one or two carefully selected forms of multimedia, you can increase your readers' interest without taking away from your written work."

Now that we've examined these possible benefits associated with using multimedia to convey thematic elements, let's take a look inside a third-grade class and check out how I prepared the students in that class to apply this writing strategy to their own narratives.

A Classroom Snapshot

As soon as I walk into the third-grade classroom where my students and I have been discussing the use of multimedia to capture thematic elements, I'm immediately thrilled by the excitement the students have for the use of this strategy.

"My theme is going to be family. There are so many great ways to show it—videos, pictures, songs!" asserts one student.

"Mine will be friendship," explains another student, "and there are also *tons* of ways of show that."

"I love how excited you all are to put this idea into action in your stories!" I address the class. "Using multimedia that shows a story's theme or main idea can be a lot of fun and can also make the story even better. As you know, the past couple of days we've been talking about this strategy. Can anyone remind us of what we did on the first day?"

"You told us what this is and showed some examples," responds a student in the front of the room.

"Absolutely right," I reply. "After I explained what this multimedia use is, I showed you two examples of student work: one about a soccer player that uses multimedia to show the theme of dedication and one about a boy who goes on an outdoor adventure that uses a photograph to help get across the theme of the power of the outdoors."

"How about yesterday?" I continue. "Who can remind us all of what we talked about in yesterday's discussion?"

"Oh, I remember," a student notes. "We talked about the benefits of doing this in writing."

"Yes," I elaborate, "we talked about how using multimedia to show thematic information and main ideas can benefit a narrative. We discussed how doing this can aid readers' comprehension of a narrative and increase their levels of engagement. Great job of recalling these ideas and helping me review them!"

"Today," I go on to say, "we're going to take an important step forward in the direction of you using this strategy in your own narratives. I'm going to give you three recommendations to keep in mind when you pick out and use multimedia in your stories to show themes and big ideas. After I explain each recommendation, I'm going to ask you why you think it's important. The first recommendation I want to give you is to make sure the multimedia you use relates to a theme or main idea in your narrative. This one's kind of self-explanatory, but it's still a really significant thing for us to think about. Sometimes when people incorporate multimedia into their writing, they want to pick the flashiest or most exciting thing they can find, but that's not always what's going to actually help your story. When looking at a form of multimedia, ask yourself, 'How does this show the theme or the main idea of my narrative?' If you can answer that question and feel good about the answer, you probably have multimedia you can use. If you can't answer it well, though, it's best to keep looking."

I look out at the classroom and see a number of nodding students. I follow up by asking them about their thoughts: "So, what do you think? Why do you think it's important to make sure the multimedia you use relates to your theme?"

"I think it's important," replies a student, "because if you use stuff that doesn't relate to your story, then you'd just have multimedia there that doesn't really help your readers."

"It could even *hurt* your readers," asserts another student, "by confusing them. If the main idea of your story is one thing and you put in a picture or video or something that has nothing to do with that thing, readers could get real confused."

"Really nicely said, both of you," I respond. "I love how you identified possible ways that using multimedia related to a theme can impact readers. Those are great insights into the importance of that idea. Now it's time for the second recommendation I have for you: Be selective when picking the multimedia you use and only include one or two examples in your narrative. Even though it can be tempting to use a whole bunch of multimedia that show your theme, I want to encourage you to be really selective and only use one or two examples of multimedia that you think show your theme really well. You can still accumulate a bunch of examples and save them in a file on your computer or bookmark the pages where you found them, but once you do that, look through them all carefully and find the one or two that you think go along with your theme perfectly. Let's hear your thoughts on this one: Why do you think it's important to be selective and only use one or two examples of multimedia in your narrative?"

"You want to pick the best examples you can find," states a student, "and if you're selective and only pick one or two great examples, that will help you pick the best ones."

"That's definitely an important part of it," I comment. "You certainly want to make sure you're using the best examples of multimedia possible so that those examples will maximize the effectiveness of your narrative. Can anyone think of any other reasons why this selectivity is important?"

"Oh, I know!" exclaims a student. "If you used a ton of multimedia, there would just be too much for the people reading. They'd look at it and be like, 'That's just too much.' They might not even read because they'd be so overwhelmed. If you just have a couple good multimedia [examples], you can help your readers without [the multimedia] taking everything over."

"Fantastic," I praise the student's response. "As you explained, it's important to make sure you don't overwhelm your reader with way too much multimedia. Now, let's think about the third and final recommendation I have for you: Make sure the multimedia you include adds to the text of your narrative without replacing it. In other words, you don't want to create a narrative that uses a lot of multimedia and not a lot of text. Any images, videos, or audio files that capture the story's theme can be a nice extra touch that helps readers understand the narrative and makes it extra engaging, but you definitely don't want it to replace the written language in the story. The multimedia is an extra part of the narrative, but not something that stands in for the actual narrative."

"What do you all think about this one?" I continue. "Why do you think it's important to use multimedia to add to a narrative instead of replacing its text?"

To my delight, a number of students' hands fly into the air. One asserts, "Because the writer still needs to write the story. Like you said, the multimedia's extra; it's not the whole thing. If it was the whole thing, it wouldn't be a written story."

"I like how you said that," I tell the student. "As you pointed out, we're still dealing with creating written pieces, and it's important to emphasize that. If a narrative is mostly multimedia, that narrative isn't a very good example of writing."

"I think it's important," states another student, "because the multimedia can only add to the story if there's enough story written there. If there isn't much written, the multimedia will take the place of the story instead of adding to it."

"That's also very nicely said," I respond. "Multimedia can only be an extra feature used to help convey a piece's theme if the author has already expressed the theme in writing. If the multimedia replaces the text instead of adding to it, the piece won't be as effective and the multimedia won't be able to support the text in the same way."

"You all did a great job of thinking about why all three of the suggestions we discussed today are important!" I say, praising the class's work. "In our next class, you'll get started applying them to your own works!"

Recommendations for Teaching Students about Incorporating Multimedia That Captures Thematic Elements

In this section, I describe a step-by-step instructional process to use when teaching students about incorporating multimedia that captures thematic elements of narrative writing. The instructional steps I recommend are (1) show students examples of narratives that use multimedia to convey thematic elements, (2) talk with students about the benefits of using multimedia to illustrate themes and main ideas, (3) provide students with specific suggestions for incorporating multimedia that captures thematic elements in their narratives, (4) meet with students as they apply this strategy to their own narratives, and (5) have students reflect on how this multimedia tool enhanced their own narratives. Each of these recommendations is described in detail in this section.

1. Show students examples of narratives that use multimedia to convey thematic elements.

This opening step gives students a concrete understanding of how multimedia can be used to convey thematic elements to a narrative's readers. When working with the third-grade class described in this chapter, I showed the students in that class examples created by my former students; this gave the third graders accessible models of how this multimedia tool can appear in practice. The first time you do this with your students, you won't have work done by your previous students to display, so I recommend either showing your students the student work example depicted in Figure 6.1 or creating your own narrative that uses multimedia to convey its theme to show your students. Then, once your students have created some examples, you can ask them for permission to use selected pieces with your future classes!

While showing students these examples, I explain that there are a variety of multimedia forms that can be used for this purpose—such as images, videos, and audio files—and that all of these have the potential to be effective. I like to tell my students that the most effective form of multimedia is the one that best fits with a particular piece. In my experience, students are eager to find multimedia online, but sometimes examples that students create themselves are best-suited to convey a certain theme or idea. In the previously described examples, the student who created the piece about a soccer player found her multimedia online, while the individual who wrote the narrative about the impact of nature used a photograph he took himself.

2. Talk with students about the benefits of using multimedia to illustrate themes and main ideas.

This second step further develops students' understanding of this multimedia tool, building on the initial knowledge established in the first step. When I talk with my students about the benefits of this strategy, I focus on how it can aid readers' comprehension and enhance their levels of engagement. I recommend conducting these discussions by first describing how using multimedia to illustrate themes and main ideas can produce these results and then identifying specific ways these benefits are achieved in the examples you previously showed them.

For example, when talking with students about how this strategy can aid readers' comprehension, I explain that multimedia that conveys a narrative's theme can help readers understand the piece by providing readers with another way to access this information: "The images, videos, or audio files an author might use to express a theme give the audience an additional way to understand the theme. The actual written text is the primary way, but the additional, or secondary, way of using multimedia to show the theme can help readers understand it even better." After sharing this information, I refer to specific ways the examples I've shown the students demonstrate this benefit, such as how the image of trees in Figure 6.1 give readers another way to understand the power of the outdoors.

In discussions of the second benefit, I explain that multimedia that conveys thematic elements can enhance readers' levels of engagement by allowing them to engage with the narrative's content in a new way. I tell the students that this benefit is similar to the previously described one in some ways, yet different in others: both give readers the chance to interact with more than just the written text, but their specific effects on readers are different. Instead of helping readers understand a text, this benefit helps readers feel more engaged and involved in it. "Clicking on a link to a song or examining a picture that has to do with a piece's theme can help readers feel involved," I tell my students. When I share this idea with my classes, I talk with them about how looking at the image in Figure 6.1 engages them in that narrative.

3. Provide students with specific suggestions for incorporating multimedia that captures thematic elements in their narratives.

Once students understand what this form of multimedia integration looks like and how it can benefit a piece of narrative writing, you can give them specific suggestions for incorporating it into their own narratives. This increases student ownership of their learning by focusing on the applicability of this concept. As discussed in this chapter's classroom snapshot, I like to provide my students with three recommendations for integrating multimedia that captures thematic elements:

◆ Make sure the multimedia relates to a theme or main idea in your narrative.
◆ Be selective when picking the multimedia you'll use, and only use one or two examples.
◆ Make sure the multimedia adds to the text without replacing it.

Like I did in the lesson illustrated in the classroom snapshot, I suggest asking students to reflect on the importance of each of these recommendations; this provides a great way to assess students' understanding of the ideas and determine their readiness to move forward in the instructional process. The students described in this chapter's snapshot were very good at discussing the importance of each of these ideas. I was particularly impressed by the student who commented on the importance of multimedia relating to the theme in a narrative by saying that readers could become very confused if this instruction was not followed. However, if my students' comments signaled confusion or misunderstanding about these recommendations, I explain the ideas further until I am confident in their awareness of what each suggestion means and why it can benefit a narrative.

4. Meet with students as they apply this strategy to their own narratives.

This fourth step further increases students' agency and responsibility, shifting from the whole-class instruction that characterizes the first three stages of the instructional process to individualized writing conferences where the teacher checks with students to see how well they're incorporating this strategy into their narratives. When I hold these conferences, I use the checklist depicted in Figure 6.2 to guide my conversations; this checklist contains three questions that are based on the recommendations discussed in the preceding section.

As I ask students these questions, I make notes about their responses and use those notes to guide the rest of the conference. In a recent conference, I met with a student who was writing a narrative about a family that bonded together during a road trip: "I'm writing about a family that was fighting a bunch but then had to take a trip together and got over [their] differences and was able to really get along," he explained. "I used a video of my family being silly and singing Disney songs to show what a family coming together can be like." This student accurately answered "yes" to all the conference questions I asked him. The multimedia he used

Figure 6.2 Conference Questions for Students Using Multimedia to Capture Thematic Elements

Questions to Ask Students during Conferences	Your Notes about Their Responses
Does the multimedia you use relate to a theme or main idea in your narrative?	
Were you selective in your multimedia use? In other words, did you pick no more than one or two examples of multimedia that perfectly go along with your theme?	
Does the multimedia you use add to the text of your narrative without replacing it?	

was certainly relevant to his theme, he only used one form of theme-based multimedia in his piece, and the video was not used to replace text in his narrative. Sometimes, students' assessments of these questions will differ from your own. I recently met with another student who said he was selective about his multimedia use, but he used four examples of multimedia, several of which conveyed the same ideas. In our conference, we talked about ways for him to be even more selective in his multimedia integration by determining what ideas each example expressed and eliminating multimedia that made redundant points. This individualized instruction is a major benefit of one-on-one writing conferences.

5. Have students reflect on how this multimedia tool enhanced their own narratives.

To effectively conclude this instructional process, I recommend asking students to think about how the strategy of using multimedia to convey thematic elements enhanced their own narratives. This final step provides a strong sense of closure to this series of activities, helping students consider how and why this multimedia tool impacted their works. I suggest guiding students' reflection by asking them two metacognition-based questions: (1) How do you think using multimedia related to your narrative's theme enhanced your narrative? (2) What do you think would be different about your narrative if you didn't use multimedia to help show its theme?

The student who used a video of his family having fun and singing together to capture the theme of a family bonding together answered the first reflection question by commenting on the concrete example and humor the multimedia he included brought to his piece: "I think the video

I used helped make my narrative really good by showing what a family coming together can be like. It also made my narrative a little funnier because the video I used is definitely funny!" His response to the second question also exhibited a strong understanding of the impact of this multimedia use, this time noting how readers might experience his work differently without it: "If I didn't use the video, the narrative wouldn't have these extra things that I think help make it better. The example and the funny video help make the story really fun to read, I think."

Final Thoughts on Incorporating Multimedia That Captures Thematic Elements

- ◆ Authors can incorporate images, videos, and audio files that reflect a theme or central idea of their narrative in some way.
- ◆ This strategy differs from the idea of using multimedia as a tool for characterization because this concept uses multimedia to convey themes or main ideas in a piece instead of using multimedia to reveal a character's personality, motivation, or interest.
- ◆ The use of multimedia that captures thematic elements can enhance students' narrative writing in two major ways:
  - ◆ It can aid readers' comprehension.
  - ◆ It can enhance their levels of engagement.
- ◆ When teaching students about using multimedia to convey thematic elements and main ideas in narrative writing,
  - ◆ Show students examples of narratives that use multimedia to convey thematic elements.
  - ◆ Talk with students about the benefits of using multimedia to illustrate themes and main ideas.
  - ◆ Provide students with specific suggestions for incorporating multimedia that captures thematic elements in their narratives.
  - ◆ Meet with students as they apply this strategy to their own narratives.
  - ◆ Have students reflect on how this multimedia tool enhanced their own narratives.

Section 4

Putting It Together

7

Assessment Strategies

While the benefits of incorporating technology into writing instruction are well supported by research (Frey, Fisher, & Gonzalez, 2010) and revealed in many teachers' accounts of their instructional experiences (Ruday, Conradi, Heny, & Lovette, 2013), the issue of assessing technology use looms large. During a recent professional development session I held on incorporating technological tools into writing instruction, several teachers raised the topic of assessing students' multimedia integration. "How do you evaluate how well students use multimedia?" one asked. "All I've ever done is just give them credit for using it, but there's got to be a better way."

This question addresses an essential idea about the nature of writing assessment in the multimedia age: the challenge of evaluating the multimedia that students use to improve their works. At the heart of the challenge is the idea that we teachers must determine what it means to use multimedia effectively, thereby requiring students to use technology strategically and not simply for the sake of doing so. In this chapter, we'll explore this challenge: each section of this chapter is dedicated to assessing students' use of one of the forms of multimedia integration described in this book. In each section, I describe what it means to use a particular multimedia tool effectively and provide a rubric for you to use with your students. (A reproducible version of each rubric can be found in Appendix A.)

Before delving into these assessment strategies, I want to make a point about how to use them: you as a teacher should decide which forms of multimedia you'd like your students to incorporate into their works. As you likely recall, this book presents two forms of multimedia integration for each of the three writing genres it addresses, describing six total multimedia uses. When teaching narrative writing, for example, you can choose whether you want to have your students use both multimedia-integration strategies described in this book related to this genre (using images, videos, and audio files as tools for characterization and incorporating multimedia that captures thematic elements) or just one of these strategies. Your decision should be based on what multimedia tools you present to your students, so that your assessment and instruction are aligned. For example, if you teach both strategies to students, I recommend asking them to include both kinds in their writing. However, if you decide to only present one of these tools in the classroom, you'll want to evaluate students on their use of that concept. With these background ideas in mind, let's now take a look at how to assess students on their use of the forms of multimedia integration described in this book.

Using Photos and Videos as Supporting Evidence in Argument Writing

When I evaluate students on their use of photos and videos to support the ideas in their argument writing, I focus on three assessment questions: (1) Is the multimedia used directly related to the content of the essay? (2) Does the multimedia highlight information that's important to the essay's argument? (3) Does this multimedia help readers visualize the essay's content? These questions, which are featured in the rubric depicted in Figure 7.1, help me evaluate whether or not a student has used this tool effectively, allowing me to generate information on the relevance and significance of the information the multimedia contains.

When I explain these evaluation criteria to my students, I emphasize the purposeful use of multimedia in writing, stating that authors should

Figure 7.1 Evaluation Criteria for Using Photos and Videos as Supporting Evidence in Argument Writing

Multimedia Use	Evaluation Criteria	Possible Points	Your Score
Using Photos and Videos as Supporting Evidence in Argument Writing	◆ Is the multimedia used directly related to the content of the essay? ◆ Does the multimedia highlight information that's important to the essay's argument? ◆ Does the multimedia help readers visualize the essay's content?	4	
Comments:			

only incorporate images and figures to support the ideas in their argument writing if those images and figures provide the benefits these questions address. Recall the example of student work featured in Chapter One, which used a photograph of public art in the author's hometown; this was an effective example of multimedia used for this purpose because it helped readers understand the impact of public art in a community and visualize what the art the author described looked like. When evaluating your students' applications of this multimedia tool, look for the same relevant, purposeful use in their argument writing.

Connecting Argument Writing Topics to Authentic Audiences through Student-Created Websites

The process of students creating their own websites to connect their argument writing topics to authentic audiences has great potential for increasing student engagement. To assess this important multimedia use, I employ three questions designed to address a site's effectiveness: (1) Does the website contain relevant features that make it visually engaging? (2) Does the site state the author's beliefs about this topic? (3) Does the site convey why its topic is important to its author? The first of these questions focuses on how well the site makes use of design components such as formatting and relevant images to help it appeal to potential readers, while the second two questions deal with how the site expresses key information about the author's argument—specifically, what the author believes and why the topic is meaningful to him or her. These evaluation questions are featured in the rubric in Figure 7.2.

Figure 7.2 Evaluation Criteria for Connecting Argument Writing Topics to Authentic Audiences through Student-Created Websites

Multimedia Use	Evaluation Criteria	Possible Points	Your Score
Connecting Argument Writing Topics to Authentic Audiences through Student-Created Websites	◆ Does the website contain relevant features that make it visually engaging? ◆ Does the site state the author's beliefs about this topic? ◆ Does the site convey why its topic is important to its author?	4	
Comments:			

Chapter Two of this book describes a student-created website that would score highly on these evaluation criteria—this site, created by the same student who used a photograph of public art in his community and featuring the same argument in favor of public art, satisfies the first component by using the site's design as well as three images of public art in the student's community to make the site visually engaging in a way that's relevant to its topic. In addition, the site scores highly on the second evaluation component because it conveys the author's stance that the public art in his community is important to its identity. Finally, the site scores highly on the third criterion because it shows the topic's importance to the author: "I am very interested in this topic because I think the public art in Charlottesville helps make the city beautiful and unique."

Creating Video Topic Trailers for Informational Writing

Video topic trailers can enhance students' experiences with informational writing, helping them interact with their topics in new ways and engage potential readers in the process. However, like all forms of multimedia that are integrated into writing instruction, this tool is most effective when taught with specific evaluation criteria in mind. When assessing my students' informational video topic trailers, I ask three assessment questions: (1) Does the trailer contain an opening statement that communicates the video's topic while also getting the reader's attention? (2) Does the trailer contain some especially significant facts about the topic? (3) Does the trailer contain visual images that introduce readers to important aspects of the topic? These questions are designed to evaluate how well the trailer introduces important information about its topic, while also capturing the viewer's attention and encouraging him or her to read the piece of informational writing that corresponds with the trailer.

In Chapter Three of this book, I describe a video topic trailer a student created to accompany an informational piece he wrote about hybrid cars. This video scores highly on the evaluation questions I use to assess this multimedia use. It satisfies the first criterion by using an engaging introduction that captures viewers' attention while communicating the topic; in this introduction, the student asks thought-provoking questions about fuel efficiency (such as "Have you ever wondered why some cars use gasoline so much faster than others?") and then introduces the topic of hybrid cars. The video scores highly on the second question by containing a number of important facts about hybrid cars in general (and the Toyota Prius in particular), identifying and explaining features such as the car's electronic motor. Finally, this topic trailer scored well on the third evaluation component because of the many visual images of the

Figure 7.3 Evaluation Criteria for Creating Video Topic Trailers for Informational Writing

Multimedia Use	Evaluation Criteria	Possible Points	Your Score
Creating Video Topic Trailers for Informational Writing	◆ Does the trailer contain an opening statement that communicates the video's topic while also getting the reader's attention? ◆ Does the trailer contain some especially significant facts about the topic? ◆ Does the trailer contain visual images that introduce readers to important aspects of the topic?	4	
Comments:			

Toyota Prius it provides, showing the car's engine, dashboard, and front. Figure 7.3 depicts the rubric I use to assess students' use of this multimedia tool.

Using Images and Figures to Aid Comprehension and Illustrate Concepts in Informational Writing

Another effective use of multimedia in informational writing is the integration of images and figures that aid comprehension and illustrate concepts; these features can highlight important details and help readers understand key ideas in a piece. When I assess students' use of this multimedia form, I use three evaluation questions related to its maximum effectiveness: (1) Do the images and/or figures used best fit with the points made in the essay? (2) Do the images and/or figures used highlight important information in the essay? (3) Does the multimedia help readers understand important information in the essay? (A rubric containing these evaluation questions is depicted in Figure 7.4.) The first question addresses the important issue of fit: an effective image or figure uses a format aligned with an essay's main points and objective. For example, an informational essay that compares two historical figures is probably best served by a figure that identifies key similarities and differences between those people, as this multimedia form reflects the essay's objective. The second question focuses on the importance of the images and figures conveying significant information: this multimedia use is only effective if the information displayed helps the audience understand the piece's topic. Finally, the third question deals with how much the images and figures can enhance readers' understanding. This evaluation component relates to the importance of using technology strategically; I tell my students that they can't simply create figures that list facts if those facts aren't helping readers understand the essay's information. They need to provide details and ideas that can aid readers' understanding, such as the order of events in someone's life or how one part of the water cycle leads to another.

Chapter Four of this book contains a student-created infographic that scores highly on each of these evaluation components. The graphic, which provides a timeline of key events in the career of retired hockey star Mario Lemieux, fits with the points made in the piece of writing because both the essay and the infographic describe significant events in Lemieux's life and how they convey his achievements. The information in this timeline highlights important details because it depicts six particularly significant events; if the timeline contained too many events or discussed some that were not especially important, it wouldn't score as highly on this category. The timeline scores highly for helping readers understand important information for similar reasons: it informs readers of especially significant

Figure 7.4 Evaluation Criteria for Using Images and Figures to Aid Comprehension and Illustrate Concepts in Informational Writing

Multimedia Use	Evaluation Criteria	Possible Points	Your Score
Using Images and Figures to Aid Comprehension and Illustrate Concepts in Informational Writing	◆ Do the images and/or figures used best fit with the points made in the essay? ◆ Do the images and/or figures used highlight important information in the essay? ◆ Does the multimedia help readers understand important information in the essay?	4	
Comments:			

details from Lemieux's life and presents them in a clear way that illustrates the progression of his career.

Using Images, Videos, and Audio Files as Tools for Characterization in Narrative Writing

The use of multimedia as a tool for characterization is an excellent example of purposeful technology integration: students can use images, videos, and audio files to help readers understand important information about a character's personality, ideas, and interests. I evaluate my students' use of this strategy with the following assessment questions: (1) Do the images, videos, and audio files you include as tools for characterization show important information about the character being described? (2) Does this multimedia help readers better understand the written descriptions of the character? (3) Is the multimedia used in a way that enhances the narrative without replacing the written description of the character? The first of these questions focuses on the idea of importance: for this strategy to be used successfully, it's essential that the information the multimedia conveys about a character is related to an important aspect of his or her identity. If a student writer uses multimedia to show something about a character that's not particularly significant to who that character is, the multimedia wouldn't be used very effectively in that case. The second and third questions both deal with the idea that images, videos, and audio files used for characterization purposes should provide readers with information that supports the written text but should not replace written descriptions of characters. These forms of multimedia can help readers better understand something that an author describes through a visual and/or auditory example of it, but shouldn't be used in a way that takes the place of its description.

Chapter Five of this book describes a number of examples of this strategy in action, including a piece in which the song "Defying Gravity" from the musical *Wicked* is used as a tool for characterization. The protagonist of this story dreams of performing on Broadway after hearing this song, so its use reveals important information about this character. In addition, the inclusion of a link to a YouTube video in the story ensures that readers can understand the reference to this song—even if they are initially unfamiliar with it. Finally, the student author did a very nice job of balancing the use of this multimedia with the written description of the character. In a first draft, her narrative included a link to this song but was lacking information about its importance to the story's protagonist. She and I discussed including a more detailed description of why "Defying Gravity" is important to the protagonist. Once the author did this, her story scored highly on this evaluation component as well. Figure 7.5 illustrates the evaluation rubric for assessing students on their use of this strategy.

Figure 7.5 Evaluation Criteria for Using Images, Videos, and Audio Files as Tools for Characterization in Narrative Writing

Multimedia Use	Evaluation Criteria	Possible Points	Your Score
Using Images, Videos, and Audio Files as Tools for Characterization in Narrative Writing	◆ Do the images, videos, and audio files you include as tools for characterization show important information about the character being described? ◆ Does the multimedia help readers better understand the written descriptions of the character? ◆ Is the multimedia used in a way that enhances the narrative without replacing the written description of the character?	4	
Comments:			

Incorporating Multimedia That Captures Thematic Elements in Narrative Writing

Multimedia can also enhance narrative writing by conveying information about the piece's theme or central idea. This multimedia use can help engage readers while also aiding their understanding of thematic information. To assess my students on their use of this strategy, I use three evaluation questions: (1) Does the multimedia used relate to a theme or main idea in the narrative? (2) Does the narrative use no more than one or two examples of multimedia that go along with its theme? (3) Does the multimedia used add to the narrative without replacing its text? The first of these questions assesses if the student has carefully chosen the multimedia for its relevance to thematic information in the narrative, or if the multimedia is used without thoughtful consideration of its relevance. The second question focuses on the amount of multimedia used in the narrative for this purpose. I tell my students that this multimedia tool is most effective if only used once or twice in the piece, as too many photos, videos, or audio files that convey a theme can overwhelm the reader. The third question

Figure 7.6 Evaluation Criteria for Incorporating Multimedia That Captures Thematic Elements in Narrative Writing

Multimedia Use	Evaluation Criteria	Possible Points	Your Score
Evaluation Criteria for Incorporating Multimedia That Captures Thematic Elements in Narrative Writing	◆ Does the multimedia used relate to a theme or main idea in the narrative? ◆ Does the narrative use no more than one or two examples of multimedia that go along with its theme? ◆ Does the multimedia used add to the narrative without replacing its text?	4	
Comments:			

evaluates how well the students use this form of multimedia in a "supporting role"—one in which the multimedia provides an additional way for readers to understand thematic information in a narrative but does not take the place of its written text.

In Chapter Six of this book, I discuss examples of student work that would score highly for this form of multimedia integration. One such example, a narrative about how experiencing the outdoors changed the protagonist's perspective on life, contains a photograph of large trees in a forest that is aligned with the piece's theme. This image is a good example of how multimedia can be used simply but effectively. Although this multimedia integration isn't particularly flashy, it nicely satisfies the evaluation criteria I use for this strategy: it relates to the piece's theme, is used selectively (so that the piece isn't weighed down with too much multimedia), and adds to the narrative without replacing any of its text. Figure 7.6 contains the assessment rubric I use for this form of multimedia integration.

Final Thoughts on Assessing Students' Use of Multimedia

◆ While there are numerous benefits associated with students incorporating multimedia in their writing, many teachers find the idea of assessing students' multimedia use challenging.

- ◆ To properly assess multimedia integration, we teachers must determine what it means to use multimedia effectively, thereby requiring students to use technology strategically and not simply for the sake of doing so.
- ◆ Each teacher should decide which forms of multimedia students should incorporate into their works.
- ◆ Make sure to evaluate your students on the multimedia tools you've presented to them so that your assessment and instruction are aligned.

8

Final Thoughts and Tips for Classroom Practice

Let's think back to the two vignettes at the beginning of this book's introductory chapter. The first one describes students in a seventh-grade English class engaged in creating websites that they'll use to share their argument essays with authentic audiences. These students explained that this form of multimedia use seems much more meaningful than other ways technology is typically integrated into their writing instruction. The second vignette recounts a conversation I had with teachers at the same school about the purposeful use of technology in writing instruction. One teacher shared that she often feels pressured to use technology as much as possible, but using technology simply for the sake of doing so didn't improve her teaching or her students' learning. She commented that the instructional approaches described in this book have helped her use multimedia in her writing instruction, with a clear understanding of the benefits of using it in those ways.

In this chapter, we'll examine some final thoughts and recommendations for incorporating multimedia into writing instruction in purposeful and thoughtful ways that maximize student learning. This chapter addresses five essential ideas, focusing on the concept that multimedia forms can be seen as tools that can make writing as effective as possible:

- Show students examples of multimedia tools used for specific purposes and explain the purposes for which they're used.
- Talk with students about how these multimedia tools enhance writing.
- Give students suggestions for effectively incorporating specific forms of multimedia in their own works.

- Confer with students as they integrate specific multimedia tools into their pieces.
- Ask students to reflect on how the multimedia they incorporated enhanced their works.

Recommendation One: Show Students Examples of Multimedia Tools Used for Specific Purposes and Explain the Purposes for Which They're Used

This opening step is crucial to the success of this instructional process, as it provides students with specific examples of multimedia tools used for particular purposes and helps them understand what those purposes are. By showing students examples of multimedia integration and explaining their purposes, you'll give your students a concrete understanding of what such a strategy can look like and why one would use it. When putting this recommendation into practice, I suggest using the examples included in this book as models of how these multimedia tools can look in action. In addition, it's always a great idea to create your own examples. This allows you to design examples directly catered to your students' ability levels and interests. Once you've shared these examples with your students, be sure to talk with them about why they are being used; for instance, when showing multimedia that supports the main point of argument evidence, you'll want to be sure that students understand what role this multimedia plays in the text. If they don't understand what effect the multimedia is meant to achieve in the piece, the examples you're showing them won't have much of an impact.

Recommendation Two: Talk with Students about How These Multimedia Tools Enhance Writing

This second step is designed to help students understand the benefits of each of the multimedia tools you've presented to them. Since the particular benefits associated with specific multimedia uses vary, the specifics of each discussion will differ; however, the important overarching idea to keep in mind is that students should understand that each multimedia use enhances writing in a certain way and authors use specific multimedia in order to achieve these benefits. For example, an author would employ the strategy of using multimedia to enhance characterization with a clear understanding of its benefits and with the goal of achieving those effects.

When talking with your students about the benefits associated with a particular multimedia use, I recommend returning to the examples you showed them in the first step of this instructional process and talking with them about what makes these multimedia forms beneficial to the pieces in which they appear. During a discussion with my students about the impact of using images and figures to aid comprehension in informational writing, I revisited the example of this concept I had shown them in our previous conversation—a humorous infographic that compares my basketball abilities with LeBron James's. Instead of using this example to show them what the concept looked like, however, I used it to provide context to our discussion of how this multimedia tool can enhance a piece of informational writing, identifying specific ways this infographic can enhance readers' experiences.

Depending on your students' attributes and preferences, you can structure these discussions in different ways: some students benefit most from their teacher explaining these benefits to them in a whole-class discussion, while others function best in a more collaborative environment in which students work in groups to discuss the benefits they believe a particular multimedia tool has. In this method, the teacher confers with each group to monitor the students' progress, and then the student groups share their ideas after groups have finished their discussions. Finally, the teacher addresses any benefits the groups didn't cover and provides any needed clarification. I typically organize these discussions in slightly more teacher-directed ways when working with younger students and release more responsibility onto the students when teaching older ones; however, I encourage you to take the specific attributes of your students into account when making these decisions with your classes.

Recommendation Three: Give Students Suggestions for Effectively Incorporating Specific Forms of Multimedia in Their Own Works

This instructional recommendation begins to gradually give increased ownership to students, as it works toward preparing them to use particular forms of multimedia in their own writing. While the specific suggestions you'll give students will vary somewhat from one multimedia use to the next, all focus in some way on using multimedia purposefully and in ways that support the written text without replacing it. Figure 8.1 depicts the specific suggestions associated with each of the forms of multimedia use described in this book.

As you discuss with your students each form of multimedia and the best ways to use it, I recommend asking them to comment on why they think each suggestion is an important idea for authors to keep in mind. This promotes discussion of the suggestions and helps you evaluate students' understanding; if some of your students aren't clear about certain suggestions, you'll want to revisit these before moving forward. Once you are comfortable with your students' level of understanding, you can move on to the next step!

Figure 8.1 Suggestions for Incorporating Multimedia Forms

Multimedia Form	Suggestions for Students Integrating It into Writing
Using photos and videos as supporting evidence in argument writing	◆ Make sure your photos and videos are directly related to the topic of your essay. ◆ Make sure that the multimedia you use highlights your most important points. ◆ Make sure that the multimedia you incorporate helps your readers visualize the topic you're describing.
Connecting argument writing to authentic audiences through student-created websites	◆ Consider ways to make your website visually engaging. ◆ Ensure that your site illustrates your beliefs about its topic. ◆ Make sure your website conveys why this topic is important to you.
Creating video topic trailers for informational writing	◆ Select some especially significant facts about your topic to share in your video topic trailer. ◆ Use a storyboard to plan the visual images you'll display in your video. ◆ Come up with a strong opening statement that you'll deliver in your video.
Using images and figures to aid comprehension and illustrate concepts in informational writing	◆ Make sure to use the kinds of images and/or figures that best fit with the points you make in your essay. ◆ Make sure the images and/or figures you use highlight important information in the essay. ◆ Make sure that the multimedia you incorporate helps readers understand important information in your essay.
Using images, videos, and audio files as tools for characterization in narrative writing	◆ Make sure that the multimedia you include shows important information about the character. ◆ Make sure that the multimedia can help readers better understand what you describe in the text. ◆ Make sure that the multimedia doesn't replace the written description in your narrative.

Figure 8.1 (Continued)

Multimedia Form	Suggestions for Students Integrating It into Writing
Incorporating multimedia that captures thematic elements in narrative writing	◆ Make sure the multimedia relates to a theme or main idea in your narrative. ◆ Be selective when picking the multimedia you'll use and only use one or two examples. ◆ Make sure the multimedia adds to the text without replacing it.

Recommendation Four: Confer with Students as They Integrate Specific Multimedia Tools into Their Pieces

This next step gives students even more ownership and responsibility, as it involves them working individually to incorporate into their writing the specific multimedia tool you've taught them. Despite this increased student ownership, however, we teachers still play important roles in this instructional stage, as it's essential for us to hold one-on-one conferences with them while they work to integrate these multimedia tools. During these conferences, I recommend asking students questions about their use of the focal strategy, based on the suggestions you shared with them in the last section. For example, here the three suggestions I give students for including multimedia as a means of characterization:

◆ Make sure to use the kinds of images and/or figures that best fit with the points you make in your essay.

◆ Make sure the images and/or figures you use highlight important information in the essay.

◆ Make sure that the multimedia you incorporate helps readers understand important information in your essay.

The corresponding conference questions I ask students when meeting with them about their use of this strategy are as follows:

◆ How does the multimedia you include show important information about the character?

◆ How does the multimedia you include help readers better understand what you describe in the text?

◆ How does the multimedia you include add to your narrative without replacing written descriptions?

Since these conference questions align with the specific suggestions I've already given my students, I can effectively evaluate how well each student with whom I confer is integrating a particular multimedia tool and revisit any aspects of that tool's use with which a student might be struggling. One-on-one conferences like these are great ways to give personalized feedback to your students.

Recommendation Five: Ask Students to Reflect on How the Multimedia They Incorporated Enhanced Their Works

I recommend concluding this instructional process by asking students to respond to reflection questions that require them to analyze the impact of specific multimedia tools on their own pieces of writing. Although some of the particular aspects of the reflection questions I ask my students vary based on the multimedia tool we're considering, the questions I present typically take two overall forms: (1) How does the multimedia use we are focusing on enhance the piece of writing? (2) How might readers' experiences be different if that multimedia form was not used? The format of these questions encourages students to think metacognitively about the impact of specific multimedia uses and what information or guidance readers wouldn't have if the author opted not to use that multimedia form. These reflection questions are designed to further help students grasp the importance of thinking carefully and critically about multimedia integration; students who can answer these questions proficiently likely have a strong understanding of the impact a particular multimedia use has on a piece of writing.

Final Thoughts on the Multimedia Writing Toolkit

While researching and writing this book, I've fielded a number of questions about its topic and what the book is designed to help teachers do. Many people with whom I spoke were accustomed to seeing technology "guidebooks" that address questions such as "How can I use PowerPoint in the classroom?" and "Should students bring their smartphones into class?" Books such as these can provide important and useful information, but I want this book to do something different that sets it apart from other books on technology integration in the classroom. I want it to emphasize the authentic and purposeful use of multimedia into student writing so that students learn how to identify the uses of specific forms of multimedia and integrate those forms into their writing to achieve particular purposes.

In my books on grammar instruction, I focus on the intentional use of specific grammatical concepts or "tools," asking questions like "What do a chainsaw and an adverb have in common?" to emphasize that both craftspeople and writers should only use certain tools when a situation calls for their use. The same idea, I believe, is applicable to the use of multimedia in student work. As I explain in this book's introduction, it's easy for "multimedia-enhanced writing" to become "writing with too much multimedia in it," but teachers can guard against this by showing students how to use multimedia thoughtfully and purposefully. If we can help our students understand the importance of purposeful multimedia use, it's likely that our students will think carefully about technology use in their future works, and perhaps we can even help them be more thoughtful and careful users of technology in all aspects of their lives.

Section **5**

Resources

References

Common Core State Standards Initiative. (2010). Common core state standards for English language arts. Retrieved from: www.corestandards.org/ELA-Literacy.

Ehmann, S., & Gayer, K. (2009). *I can write like that! A guide to mentor texts and craft studies for writers' workshop, K-6.* Newark, DE: International Reading Association.

Fletcher, R., & Portalupi, J. (2001). *Writing workshop: The essential guide.* Portsmouth, NH: Heinemann.

Frey, N., Fisher, D., & Gonzalez, A. (2010). *Literacy 2.0: Reading and writing in 21st century classrooms.* Bloomington, IN: Solution Tree.

Katzman, R. (2016). A record-setting tunnel. *Time for Kids.* Retrieved from: http://www.timeforkids.com/news/record-setting-tunnel/431551.

Knoester, M. (2009). Inquiry into urban adolescent independent reading habits: Can Gee's theory of discourses provide insight? *Journal of Adolescent & Adult Literacy*, 52(8), 676–685.

Lenhart, A., Madden, M., & Hitlin, P. (2005). *Teens and technology: Youth are leading the transition to a fully wired and mobile nation.* Washington, DC: PEW Internet and Family Life.

Ruday, S. (2011). Expanding the possibilities of discussion: A strategic approach to using online discussion boards in the middle and high school English classroom. *Contemporary Issues in Technology and Teacher Education*, 11(4), 350–361.

Ruday, S. (2015). *The argument writing toolkit: Using mentor texts in grades 6–8.* New York, NY: Routledge.

Ruday, S., Conradi, K., Heny, N., & Lovette, G. (2013). " 'You can't put the Genie back into the bottle': English teachers' beliefs and attitudes regarding digital literacies in the classroom." In P. J. Dunston, S. K. Fullerton, C. C. Bates, P. M. Stecker, M. W. Cole, A. H. Hall, D. Herro, and K. N. Headley (Eds.) *62nd Yearbook of the Literacy Research Association* (199–215). Altamonte Springs, FL: Literacy Research Association.

Wolsey, T. D., & Grisham, P. D. L. (2012). *Transforming writing instruction in the digital age: Techniques for grades 5–12.* New York, NY: Guilford Press.

Young, C. A., & Bush, J. (2004). Teaching the English language arts with technology: A critical approach and pedagogical framework. *Contemporary Issues in Technology and Teacher Education*, 4(1), 1–22.

Appendix A
Reproducible Charts and Forms You Can Use in Your Classroom

This appendix contains reproducible versions of key charts and forms featured in this book. It is designed to help you put the ideas in this book into action in your classroom.

Figure 1.3 Analysis Questions for Integrating Multimedia

Summary of multimedia you are considering	
Is this multimedia directly related to the content of your essay?	
Does this multimedia highlight important information in your essay?	
Does this multimedia help readers visualize the topic of your essay?	

© 2017, *The Multimedia Writing Toolkit*, Sean Ruday, Taylor & Francis

Figure 2.3 Guideline Chart for Creating Websites

Guideline Question	Your Response	Evidence That Supports Your Response
Does your website contain features that make it visually engaging?		
Does your site state your beliefs about its topic?		
Does your site convey why its topic is important to you?		

© 2017, *The Multimedia Writing Toolkit*, Sean Ruday, Taylor & Francis

Figure 3.2 Conference Questions for Students Creating Video Topic Trailers

Questions to Ask Students during Conferences	Your Notes about Their Responses
What are some especially significant facts about your topic that you decided to share in your video topic trailer? Follow-up question: Why do you feel those facts are especially important?	
Which visual images will you display in your video topic trailer? Follow-up question: Why did you choose these scenes?	
What opening statement will you deliver in your video topic trailer? Follow-up question: How does that opening statement communicate the video's topic while also getting the reader's attention?	

© 2017, *The Multimedia Writing Toolkit*, Sean Ruday, Taylor & Francis

Figure 5.2 Conference Questions for Students Using Multimedia to Enhance Characterization

Questions to Ask Students during Conferences	Your Notes about Their Responses
How does the multimedia you include show important information about the character?	
How does the multimedia you include help readers better understand what you describe in the text?	
How does the multimedia you include add to your narrative without replacing written descriptions?	

© 2017, *The Multimedia Writing Toolkit*, Sean Ruday, Taylor & Francis

Figure 6.2 Conference Questions for Students Using Multimedia to Capture Thematic Elements

Questions to Ask Students during Conferences	Your Notes about Their Responses
Does the multimedia you use relate to a theme or main idea in your narrative?	
Were you selective in your multimedia use? In other words, did you pick no more than one or two examples of multimedia that perfectly go along with your theme?	
Does the multimedia you use add to the text of your narrative without replacing it?	

© 2017, *The Multimedia Writing Toolkit*, Sean Ruday, Taylor & Francis

Figure 7.1 Evaluation Criteria for Using Photos and Videos as Supporting Evidence in Argument Writing

Multimedia Use	Evaluation Criteria	Possible Points	Your Score
Using Photos and Videos as Supporting Evidence in Argument Writing	◆ Is the multimedia used directly related to the content of the essay? ◆ Does the multimedia highlight information that's important to the essay's argument? ◆ Does the multimedia help readers visualize the essay's content?	4	

Comments:

© 2017, *The Multimedia Writing Toolkit*, Sean Ruday, Taylor & Francis

Figure 7.2 Evaluation Criteria for Connecting Argument Writing Topics to Authentic Audiences through Student-Created Websites

Multimedia Use	Evaluation Criteria	Possible Points	Your Score
Connecting Argument Writing Topics to Authentic Audiences through Student-Created Websites	◆ Does the website contain relevant features that make it visually engaging? ◆ Does the site state the author's beliefs about this topic? ◆ Does the site convey why its topic is important to its author?	4	

Comments:

© 2017, *The Multimedia Writing Toolkit*, Sean Ruday, Taylor & Francis

Figure 7.3 Evaluation Criteria for Creating Video Topic Trailers for Informational Writing

Multimedia Use	Evaluation Criteria	Possible Points	Your Score
Creating Video Topic Trailers for Informational Writing	◆ Does the trailer contain an opening statement that communicates the video's topic while also getting the reader's attention? ◆ Does the trailer contain some especially significant facts about the topic? ◆ Does the trailer contain visual images that introduce readers to important aspects of the topic?	4	

Comments:

© 2017, *The Multimedia Writing Toolkit*, Sean Ruday, Taylor & Francis

Figure 7.4 Evaluation Criteria for Using Images and Figures to Aid Comprehension and Illustrate Concepts in Informational Writing

Multimedia Use	Evaluation Criteria	Possible Points	Your Score
Using Images and Figures to Aid Comprehension and Illustrate Concepts in Informational Writing	◆ Do the images and/ or figures used best fit with the points made in the essay? ◆ Do the images and/ or figures used highlight important information in the essay? ◆ Does the multimedia help readers understand important information in the essay?	4	

Comments:

© 2017, *The Multimedia Writing Toolkit*, Sean Ruday, Taylor & Francis

Figure 7.5 Evaluation Criteria for Using Images, Videos, and Audio Files as Tools for Characterization in Narrative Writing

Multimedia Use	Evaluation Criteria	Possible Points	Your Score
Using Images, Videos, and Audio Files as Tools for Characterization in Narrative Writing	◆ Do the images, videos, and audio files you include as tools for characterization show important information about the character being described? ◆ Does the multimedia help readers better understand the written descriptions of the character? ◆ Is the multimedia used in a way that enhances the narrative without replacing the written description of the character?	4	

Comments:

© 2017, *The Multimedia Writing Toolkit*, Sean Ruday, Taylor & Francis

Figure 7.6 Evaluation Criteria for Incorporating Multimedia that Captures Thematic Elements in Narrative Writing

Multimedia Use	Evaluation Criteria	Possible Points	Your Score
Evaluation Criteria for Incorporating Multimedia That Captures Thematic Elements in Narrative Writing	◆ Does the multimedia used relate to a theme or main idea in the narrative? ◆ Does the narrative use no more than one or two examples of multimedia that go along with its theme? ◆ Does the multimedia use add to the narrative without replacing its text?	4	

Comments:

© 2017, *The Multimedia Writing Toolkit*, Sean Ruday, Taylor & Francis

Appendix B
A Guide for Book Studies

The Multimedia Writing Toolkit is ideally suited for groups of elementary and middle school teachers who are interested in helping their students incorporate multimedia into their writing in ways that are both purposeful and engaging and who want to work together as a book-study group. If you are using this text for a book study, I recommend you and your group members reflect on important issues in the book at three distinct stages: before reading, during reading, and after reading. The following sections provide key points to consider before examining the text, while you're reading it, and once you've completed it.

Before Reading
Before reading this text, I suggest activating your prior knowledge of this book's central points by considering these key ideas:

◆ How have you incorporated technology into your writing instruction?
◆ Of these forms of technology integration, which have struck you as most successful? Why?
◆ What are some forms of technology integration you've used in your writing instruction that have not been particularly successful? Why do you believe this is?
◆ How would you describe your beliefs on teaching with technology?

During Reading
After reading the book's introductory chapter, answer the following questions:

◆ What did you notice about the description at the beginning of the book of students creating websites they'll use to share their argument essays?
◆ Early in the introduction, we meet a teacher named Kimberly who described both opportunities and challenges associated with incorporating technology into her instruction. What are some comments she makes to which you can relate?

Next, I recommend answering the two questions below with your book group members at the conclusion of each chapter between Chapter One and Chapter Six:

- How can the multimedia use described in this chapter enhance a piece of writing?
- What are some specific adaptations to the ideas and recommendations described in this chapter that you'd make when teaching your students about its topic?

Next, read Chapter Seven and discuss the following questions with the other members of your book-study group:

- What are some challenges you believe exist when it comes to evaluating students' multimedia use?
- Why do you think it's important to align instruction and assessment when evaluating students' use of multimedia in their writings?
- What are some benefits that can come from separately evaluating each aspect of effective multimedia use?

Next, read Chapter Eight and discuss the following with your group members:

- How do you feel the ideas discussed in Chapter Eight work together to create strong multimedia-infused writing instruction?

After Reading

Now that you've finished *The Multimedia Writing Toolkit*, talk with your book-study group about your responses to these four questions:

- How did the ideas in this book enhance your understanding of how to use multimedia in writing instruction?
- Why do you think this book emphasizes the purposeful use of multimedia integration so much?
- Which of the multimedia tools described in this book do you see as having the greatest relevance to your students' interests and ability levels?
- Reflection is a major part of this book; students reflect on the importance of each multimedia tool after using it in their works. How will you help your students reflect on the multimedia forms you teach them?
- What is one way you feel this book will immediately impact the way you integrate technology into your writing instruction?

© 2017, *The Multimedia Writing Toolkit*, Sean Ruday, Taylor & Francis

Appendix C
Links to Web Content

This Appendix contains links to some key web-based content discussed in this book, including a website discussed in Chapter Two that illustrates an example of how authors can share their argument essays with interested audiences and the video discussed in Chapter Three that provides an example of a video topic trailer.

- ◆ Website, "The Importance of Parents Reading to their Children": http://readtochildren.weebly.com/
- ◆ Video Topic Trailer on Hybrid Cars: https://www.youtube.com/watch?v=yaC9FcSD7H4
- ◆ Website, "Time for Kids": http://www.timeforkids.com/
- ◆ "Time for Kids" Article, "A Record-Setting Tunnel": http://www.timeforkids.com/news/record-setting-tunnel/431551

© 2017, *The Multimedia Writing Toolkit*, Sean Ruday, Taylor & Francis

Taylor & Francis eBooks

Helping you to choose the right eBooks for your Library

Add Routledge titles to your library's digital collection today. Taylor and Francis ebooks contains over 50,000 titles in the Humanities, Social Sciences, Behavioural Sciences, Built Environment and Law.

Choose from a range of subject packages or create your own!

Benefits for you

» Free MARC records
» COUNTER-compliant usage statistics
» Flexible purchase and pricing options
» All titles DRM-free.

REQUEST YOUR **FREE** INSTITUTIONAL TRIAL TODAY

Free Trials Available
We offer free trials to qualifying academic, corporate and government customers.

Benefits for your user

» Off-site, anytime access via Athens or referring URL
» Print or copy pages or chapters
» Full content search
» Bookmark, highlight and annotate text
» Access to thousands of pages of quality research at the click of a button.

eCollections – Choose from over 30 subject eCollections, including:

Archaeology	Language Learning
Architecture	Law
Asian Studies	Literature
Business & Management	Media & Communication
Classical Studies	Middle East Studies
Construction	Music
Creative & Media Arts	Philosophy
Criminology & Criminal Justice	Planning
Economics	Politics
Education	Psychology & Mental Health
Energy	Religion
Engineering	Security
English Language & Linguistics	Social Work
Environment & Sustainability	Sociology
Geography	Sport
Health Studies	Theatre & Performance
History	Tourism, Hospitality & Events

For more information, pricing enquiries or to order a free trial, please contact your local sales team: www.tandfebooks.com/page/sales

 Routledge
Taylor & Francis Group

The home of Routledge books

www.tandfebooks.com

Lightning Source UK Ltd.
Milton Keynes UK
UKOW05f0310211117
313075UK00013B/641/P

9 781138 200111